COMMUNICATIONS RECEIVERS

THE VACUUM TUBE ERA: 50 GLORIOUS YEARS

1932-1981

COMPLETELY REVISED SECOND EDITION

BY

RAYMOND S. MOORE

RSM COMMUNICATIONS
WALPOLE, MASS, USA

First Edition, First Printing, May 1987
          Second Printing, Revised, May 1988
Second Edition, New and Revised, September 1991

Printed in the United States of America.

ISBN 0-9618882-1-0

RSM COMMUNICATIONS
P O BOX 218
NORWOOD, MASS 02062

PREFACE

When I published the first edition of this book I had no idea how it would sell. Apparently the book met a need which had never been filled before because the first small printing sold out and a second, professionally produced, printing sold out almost a year ago. At that time I had to decide whether to reprint the original book or to completely revise it and come out with a new, second edition.

Eventually the decision was made to incorporate all the new information I had received from many readers and other sources and to change the format to include a picture of every receiver. This last had been requested by many readers of the first edition. It turned out to be a tremendous job made a little easier by the detailed card file compiled during the writing of the first edition and continually updated since.

This is the second and final edition of the book. Perhaps a supplement sometime in the future but it is time to move on to other projects. Maybe the next project will be a similar book on transmitters or on regenerative receivers or on solid state receivers?

The book is the by-product of a lifetime search for the ULTIMATE RECEIVER. The search not only led me to my career as an engineer and executive in the vacuum tube and semiconductor industries but produced a large reservoir of information which was collected as I analyzed just about every receiver ever built trying to extract the secret ingredients which could produce the ULTIMATE RECEIVER. Of course, the search revealed that there are no magic circuits or secret ingredients and there is no universal ULTIMATE RECEIVER. Every one who admires and uses receivers sees a different ULTIMATE RECEIVER in his mind.

GUIDELINES

The guidelines for including a receiver remain the same as for the first edition but are more rigorously adhered to in order to hold the book within manageable limits. For example, most of the consumer and entertainment products of Hallicrafters and National have been eliminated. There were numerous requests to add other receivers, long wave, VHF, military, et al, but I had to draw the line somewhere.

1. Superheterodynes only.

2. Manufactured in the USA.

3. Offered for sale to radio amateurs and the general public.

4. Vacuum tube receivers only.

5. Must have a BFO.

6. Continuous tuning - excludes switch tuned and fixed tuned receivers.

7. Covers all or part of the high frequency bands.

8. Advertised or promoted for communications use.

CHANGES

The first chapter on the history of the communications receiver industry is unchanged from the first edition because no significant new information became available. The histories of many companies, however, have been revised and enlarged as the result of much new information. I believe these histories are the most complete and accurate ever published. This is especially true of Hallicrafters where much of the previously published information is a combination of myths and misinformation. Other companies with significant new information are E. M. Sargent, McMurdo

Silver, Inc., and Patterson. A few new companies have been added, Barrett Manufacturing, Boulevard Electronics, McCulla Manufacturing, Norden Labs, Pierson-DeLane.

The quality of photos used in the book range from good to very bad. Most I consider to be good but occasionally I have used a poor photo in order to make the book as complete as possible.

ACKNOWLEDGEMENTS

I approach this section with some trepidation because I am sure to overlook some who have made contributions and to understate the contribution of others.

H. L. Chadbourne who spent many years researching the communications receiver industry for a book, which he was never able to complete, was totally unselfish and enthusiastic in contributing new information to me. Floyd A. Paul is a leading expert on the radio manufacturers of the Los Angeles area and is largely responsible for the new information on Patterson and Pierson-DeLane. Robert E. Samuelson contributed valuable information which made it possible to piece together the early history of Hallicrafters and Echophone. Douglas E. Lyon, Robert J. Hopkins, Jr., and Fred Hammond, VE3HC, contributed significantly.

Others who contributed and deserve more space than I can give them are Larry P. Waggoner, Reinhold Fiedler, John L. Orahood, Walter Hann, OE8WHK, Dave Sutton, WA9J, John Bryant, Richard W. Parker, David Burke, James T. Hanlon, H. Miller, Chien Chung Chien, Darryl Kasch, John W. Gibson, K9KRW, Richard R. George, W0TRF, Jack Woods, Michael Harla, John White, Stuart Meyer, James A. Maxwell, W6CF, John Nagle, Dan A. Unruh, Jim Musgrove, K5BZH.

Many thanks also to my new fiancee, Marty, who has plunged in and helped me in this little business. Without her this book would still be months away.

CHAPTER I

HISTORY OF THE COMMUNICATIONS RECEIVER

A revolution occurred during the first half of the 1930's in the receiving equipment used for communications and monitoring work on the high frequencies.

Table I was compiled from station descriptions in the pages of QST. In 1931 78% (35 of 45) of the receivers used in amateur stations were homebuilt compared with 20% (7 of 35) only five years later in 1936. The type of receiver also changed markedly. In 1931 89% (40 of 45) of the receivers used regenerative detectors. By 1936 only 23% (8 of 35) of the hams used regenerative receivers.

pared to the communications receivers we became accustomed to during the next 40 years. They lacked direct calibration, bandswitching, IF filters and the indispensable "S" meter.

Perhaps the first complete, modern communications receiver was the RME-9 which was introduced in December, 1933. It set the standard for most of the communications receivers built well into the post-World-War II period. It had a directly calibrated airplane dial with mechanical bandspread, bandswitching, an "R" meter, RF amplification, AVC.

AMATEUR STATION RECEIVERS			
1931		1936	
No.	Type of Receiver	No.	Type of Receiver
17	Homebuilt Regen Det/Audio	5	National HRO
14	Homebuilt RF/Regen Det/Audio	4	National FB-7
4	National SW-5 (Regen)	4	RME-69
4	Homebuilt Superhet	4	Homebuilt RF/Regen Det/Audio
3	Pilot Super Wasp (Regen)	3	Hallicrafters S/SX-6
2	Grebe CR-18 (Regen)	3	Hammarlund Comet Pro
1	Silver-Marshall Superhet	2	RCA ACR-136
		2	RME-9D
		2	Homebuilt Regen Det/Audio
		1	National SW-3
		1	RCA ACR-175
		1	Homebuilt Superhet
		1	Patterson PR-10
		1	Pilot Super Wasp (Regen)
		1	Hammarlund Super Pro

TABLE I

The first rudimentary communications receiver was the Hammarlund "Comet" introduced late in 1931. An improved "Comet Pro" followed in the spring of 1932. A more advanced receiver, the National AGS appeared in July, 1932.

But these receivers were crude com-

It is interesting that RME continued to make this same receiver, circuit-wise, until 1953. The RME-50 which was last manufactured in that year had exactly the same circuit configuration as the RME-9, RF amplifier, mixer, HFO, two IF amplifiers, detector, BFO, two audio amplifiers and a rectifier. Indeed, the RME-50 even

TABLE II — COMMUNICATIONS RECEIVER CHRONOLOGY — DATE / MANUFACTURER & MODEL	RF Amplifier	Calibrated Dial	Bandspread	Ant Trimmer	AVC	Crystal Filter	Bandswitching	"R" Meter	Double Conversion
1932 Jan Hammarlund "Comet"									
Apr Hammarlund "Comet Pro"			●						
Oct National AGS	●		●		●				
Dec Hendricks & Harvey Custom (Var 1)			●			●		●	
1933 Feb McMurdo Silver 3A	●		●						
Mar Lincoln R9					●		●	●	
Mar National FB-7			●						
Mar Leeds Supreme (Kit)	●				●	●			
Mar Hendricks & Harvey Custom (Var 2)	●				●	●		●	
Apr National FBX			●			●			
Jul National AGS-X	●		●		●	●			
Sep McMurdo Silver 5A	●		●		●		●		
Sep Ross 2B			●		●		●		
Nov Hammarlund "Comet-Pro" (Var 4-7)			●		●	●			
Nov Postal International	●		●						
Dec RME-9	●	●	●		●	●	●	●	
1934 Jan McMurdo Silver 5B	●		●		●	●			
Jan Ross Jupiter			●		●		●		
Feb Sargent 9-33			●	●			●		●
Mar Patterson PR-10			●	●	●		●		
Jun RME-9D	●	●	●	●	●	●		●	
Sep Sargent 8-34			●	●	●	●		●	
Oct Patterson PR-12 (Deliv. 6/35)	●		●	●	●	●		●	
Oct Hallicrafters Super Skyrider	●	●	●		●	●	●	●	
Oct National HRO	●		●		●	●		●	
Oct McMurdo Silver 5C	●	●	●		●	●	●		
Nov Sargent All-Wave Explorer					●		●		
Nov Postal 35	●	●	●		●			●	
Dec RCA ACR-136	●	●	●		●		●		

had the single knob tuning with mechanical bandspread of the RME-9. RME had gone to the two dial, electrical bandspread system with the RME-9D in mid-1934 but returned to the mechanical bandspread system for good in 1941 with the RME-41 and -43 models.

Table II presents a chronological look at the development of the communications receiver from 1932 through 1934. You knew that the communications receiver really arrived when RCA entered the market in December, 1934.

What triggered this revolution which brought the communications receiver from the dark ages to the mid-twentieth century in less than five years?

Much of the impetus came from the growth of amateur radio and from their organization the American Radio Relay League. In June, 1932, James Lamb, technical editor of the ARRL's publication, QST, published an article in QST which established the guidelines for the communications receivers of the next several decades.

The article, "What's Wrong With Our CW Receivers?", showed that the broad tuning and unstable regenerative receivers then used by most amateurs had not kept pace with the contemporary crystal-controlled and well filtered transmitters.

Lamb's next article in the August, 1932, QST described an advanced receiving system. The article, "Short-Wave Receiver To Match Present Conditions", was subtitled "Constructional and Operating Features of the "Single-Signal Superhet." It covered the basic receiver principles of selectivity, frequency stability and sensitivity and gave techniques and circuits achieving them. He used a crystal filter for single-signal CW reception and showed how to stabilize the high frequency oscillator. The principles of quiet and electrically stable RF amplifiers were also covered.

By December, 1932, an advertisement for the first commercial receiver with a crystal filter appeared and within a year Lamb's recommendations were standard in better quality receivers.

At the same time, shortwave reception was becoming a craze with the general public which spurred developments in the broadcast receiver industry. Many receivers during this period had at least one shortwave band and some were quite advanced with features not found in the few available communications receivers. Single dial tuning, direct calibration, bandswitching, AVC, RF amplification, even double conversion were used in broadcast receivers. This demand for efficient, convenient shortwave reception accelerated the development of better components and circuits which were also useful to the communications receiver designer.

Indeed, a number of the communications receivers of the mid-1930's were little more than broadcast receivers repackaged in metal communications-type cabinets. The Hallicrafters Super-7 (c. 1935), for example, had a small seven tube chassis which occupied only half the impressive cabinet.

During 1933 and 1934 a dozen manufacturers turned out communications receivers. We have already mentioned RME, National and Hammarlund. The last of the "Big Four" manufacturers of the 1930's, Hallicrafters, didn't bring out their first superheterodyne communications receiver until the fall of 1934. Previously they had made custom broadcast receivers and a TRF regenerative shortwave receiver.

Communication receiver developments accelerated and reached a peak in 1935. Public interest in shortwave reception also continued to surge toward a peak and the result was the availability of higher performance components making for higher performance receivers. Improved insulation for bandswitches and coils, metal and acorn tubes which reduced input loading for efficient RF amplification and iron core IF transformers all were designed into receivers during 1935.

Hallicrafters was particularly dynamic in adopting new components, twice revamping their line in 1935. In January the company replaced the original Super Skyrider with three new models, the S4, S5 and S6, differing from each other only in frequency coverage. These were replaced in September with the SX-9 Super Skyrider, the first communications receiver to use metal tubes and iron core IF transformers. The Super Skyrider series went on to include the SX-11, SX-16, SX-17, SX-28 and the SX-28A which was produced until 1946. Beginning in 1936 Hallicrafters added additional models to fill out their line which included the $29.50 Sky Buddy at the low end and the Super Skyrider at the high end.

Other new receivers to appear in 1935 were the McMurdo Silver 5D, RCA AR-60, Patterson PR-16, Breting 12, Sargent 20 and RME-69. Tobe Deutschman marketed two communications receiver kits. one covered the amateur bands only while the second was general coverage. Both used the "Tobe Tuner" pre-wired front end.

Outside of improved components the

communications receiver remained essentially unchanged from the RME-9 in 1933 until after World War II. Although single sideband, lattice filters, double conversion and most of the other modern refinements were available and, indeed, in use by the communications companies, they were not used in amateur communications receivers.

Everyone made the same receiver dressed a little differently. Almost every communications receiver from 1933 to the late 1940's had one or two RF stages, a mixer, high frequency oscillator, a crystal filter, two or three IF amplifiers, a second detector, BFO and a couple of stages of audio. At the low end of the line they eliminated the RF amplifiers, combined the mixer and HFO and dropped down to one IF amplifier.

The major receiver manufacturers could be divided into two groups in the 1930's. One group, led by Hallicrafters and including RME and Howard, specialized in giving the most features per dollar. They did this by using mostly purchased, standard components, especially the high-volume, low-priced parts developed for the all wave broadcast sets.

The other group of manufacturers which included National and Hammarlund custom designed and manufactured the key components for their receivers. This included tuning capacitors, IF transformers, coils, band changing systems and tuning mechanisms.

National was particularly protective of their quality image. When, in 1937, they brought out the medium-priced NC-80 series they were apologetic. Their advertisement said, "Most amateurs do not need to be told that when a communications receiver is to be sold for as low a price as the NC-80X it is necessary to make compromises."

The Hallicrafters Sky Buddy at $29.50 was a big seller during the depression ridden 1930's. Several models were manufactured from 1936 to 1942 and over 15,000 were built. It was the basic super-heterodyne circuit stripped bare. The tube count was reduced to five (six in the S-19R) by using multi-purpose tubes and eliminating the RF amplifier and one IF amplifier. There was no filter. Although the insides were minimal the outside looked like a real communications receiver with its large dial and multitude of knobs and switches. And it could perform when conditions weren't too tough. Many a ham and SWL has fond memories of the Sky Buddy.

At the other end of the scale the National HRO seemed doomed as an anachronism before it ever appeared. Electrically, the HRO was almost the same as the RME-9 with one additional RF amplifier. But it used plug-in coils, did not have direct calibration and had a separate power supply. Yet it became one of the most successful receivers ever introduced, remaining in production basically unchanged until 1949 and with modifications until 1964. What it had was uncompromising mechanical design. The famous PW dial and its gear system, the custom four-gang variable capacitor and the four-gang, plug-in coil system were all a reflection of the mechanical engineering background of James Millen, National's chief engineer.

Another top-of-the-line receiver which lasted well into the solid-state era was the Hammarlund Super-Pro. Hammarlund started design of the ultimate receiver, the Comet Super Pro, to replace the Comet Pro, in 1933. Like National their design approach was uncompromising. They designed a unique bandswitching mechanism, special IF transformers with variable coupling and a custom twelve gang tuning capacitor. It was scheduled for release in early 1935. The project did not go smoothly, however, and it was 1936 before the receiver was ready for delivery. It turned out to be the most long lived of all receiver designs. Minor changes occurred in 1937 (SP-100), 1939 (SP-200, and 1945 (SP-400). In 1949 (SP-600) double conversion, turret coil changing and an internal power supply were added. The SP-600 continued to be sold until 1972.

Perhaps the most ambitious communications receiver manufactured during the pre-war years was the Hallicrafters DD-1 Skyrider Diversity. It was a 25 tube dual diversity receiving system - two separate receivers on a single chassis with a common HFO. A separate power supply sat on one side of the receiver and a separate audio chassis on the other, all usually shown atop a huge Jensen console speaker. At a time when the SX-17 Super Skyrider cost $137.50 the DD-1 went for $550. Only about 500 DD-1's were built during 1938 and 1939.

In 1940 Hallicrafters introduced the last of the Super Skyrider models, the SX-28. This was their ultimate refinement of the conventional, straight superheterodyne. The SX-28 used 15 tubes and included the Lamb noise silencer circuit. The receiver was used extensively by the military and Hallicrafters produced 50,000 during World War II. The SX-28A, with some minor refinements, was produced until 1946 when Hallicrafters introduced their post-war models.

All-wave broadcast receivers reached the height of ostentation and complexity in the second half of the 1930's. The zenith of the genre was in 1937 when E. H. Scott introduced his Philharmonic XXX, a 30 tube, chrome plated set which full page ads proclaimed to be the "World's Most Powerful Radio." At the same time McMurdo Silver touted his 21 tube Masterpiece VI as the "Finest Receiver Ever Built."

To complete the story of the 1930's we must mention some of the people involved with the development of the communications receiver. McMurdo Silver may have been the most familiar name of the '30's. He was president of Silver-Marshall which went bankrupt in 1931 and eventually became Hallicrafters. Then he became president of McMurdo-Silver, Inc., which lasted until 1938 when the company went bankrupt. In 1938-39 he was an engineer for E. I. Guthman. During all this time he was a prolific writer for the popular technical magazines of the time, appearing almost monthly with an article about his latest receiver design.

Bill Halligan of Hallicrafters and E. H. Scott were frequently pictured in their company's advertisements Scott also made a number of well publicized trips to his native New Zealand. Halligan was a gregarious man who was often photographed at radio conventions. Karl Miles and Kendall Clough of Hallicrafters engineering wrote a number of articles about new technical developments. James Millen of National was another prolific writer and Lloyd Hammarlund was often quoted and pictured in magazines.

During World War II the major receiver manufacturers worked around the clock producing communications equipment for the armed services. Hallicrafters turned out tens of thousands of SX-28, S-29 portables, S-27/S-36 (BC-787) VHF receivers, and SCR-299 communications systems containing the BC-610 (HT-4) transmitter and the BC-642 receiver.

National and Hammarlund produced versions of their top receivers, the HRO and Super Pro, for the military in large quantities. RME turned out signal generators and shipboard communications equipment.

THE FIRST POSTWAR DECADE

With World War II the communications reciver business changed forever. Gone were Howard, Breting, Patterson, RCA, Sargent, Meissner and Guthman. Gone were the highly visible engineers and entrepreneurs. Big business methods prevailed and receivers became the product of engineering teams working in anonymity in obscure laboratories. Also, communications receivers became a minor part of the business at the surviving companies such as National, Hammarlund and Hallicrafters. The money was in the military business.

During the war communications receiver manufacturers teased us with hints of secret wartime developments that would dramatically improve receivers after the war. What a disappointment! The postwar sets were the prewar sets not even thinly disguised. About the only wartime development utilized was the miniature tube (6AK5, 6AG5) which appeared late in 1946 in the Hallicrafters SX-42 and the Collins 75A. National's HRO-5 and Hammarlund's new SP-400 Super Pro still used the prewar metal tubes.

The first postwar receiver to depart significantly from the 1933 RME-9 circuit was the Collins 75A in October 1946. This receiver introduced the multi-conversion, fixed HFO circuit which eventually became the basis for most quality receivers well into the 1980's, until the step-tuned, fully synthesized receiver took over. In the 75A the HFO was crystal controlled and the tuning done with a permeability tuned VFO. The result was a degree of frequency stability and readout accuracy never before approached.

The 75A was Collins' first venture into the general communications receiver market. The 75A evolved through the 75A-4 and then into the smaller 75S series which continued in production until the mid-1970's. The general coverage 51-J series evolved from the 75A as did, eventually, the R-390 series, perhaps the ultimate vacuum tube receivers.

Other receivers in the immediate postwar period retained prewar circuitry until the 1950's. The Hallicrafters SX-42, National HRO-5, Hammarlund SP-400 and the RME-45 were only slightly changed from the 1930's models. Two new companies entered the communications receiver market. The Pierson KP-81 and the Cardwell 54 were conventional, straight superheterodynes and neither lasted very long.

Hallicrafters maintained their prewar tradition of manufacturing a broad line of receivers for every purse. The S-38 replaced the low end S-19 Sky Buddy although inflation nudged the price up from the traditional $29.50 to $39.50. The S-38 eventually evolved into the S-38E which lasted until 1961 and sold for $54.95. The S-40 was a repackaged S-20 Sky Champion and lasted through a number of revisions until 1954.

Eventually the first postwar decade did produce dramatic changes in communications receiver design and much of the credit for this must go to the ARRL's campaign for increased use of SSB by amateurs. They had been pushing better selectivity for some time to reduce heterodyne interference on the congested phone bands and in 1948 went all the way and advocated SSB, thus eliminating the source of the heterodynes.

Point-to-point communications companies had been using SSB for years but their cumbersome, complex, custom made equipment was not suitable for amateur use. So the techniques, components and circuits had to be developed to make SSB practical for general use. The frequency stability of postwar receivers (except the 75A) were grossly inadequate. Much better selectivity was required for both sideband generation and reception. A different approach to AVC was needed.

Collins became heavily involved in SSB, not only for amateurs, but for commercial and military applications. They had already shown the way to adequate frequency stability with fixed HFO, tunable VFO approach of the 75A.

In 1952 Collins announced another revolutionary development, the mechanical filter. With its flat top and steep sides, in a compact package, the mechanical filter was the perfect component for SSB generation and reception. Until then most receivers used Lamb's 1932 single series-resonant crystal with its peaked nose and drooping skirts.

Another method of obtaining a near-optimum selectivity curve is with cascaded L/C circuits at a low intermediate frequency. McLaughlin described 50 kHz IF amplifiers for single sideband reception of AM signals in QST in 1941 and 1947. In 1948 McMurdo Silver manufactured an IF amplifier with eight 100 kHz tuned circuits which had nearly ideal selectivity.

Hallicrafters was the first to integrate the low frequency, cascaded IF system into a receeiver. In 1951 Hallicrafters introduced a 50 kHz IF system in the S-76 receiver, an arrangement they would continue to use in their top receivers for the next 15 years. It used a number of 50 kHz high-Q tuned circuits which had a very narrow, steep sided selectivity curve when they were all peaked on the same frequency. By switching in capacitors to detune the circuits, and resistors to spoil the Q, the passband was widened for phone reception.

The quest for selectivity regressed a bit with the popularization of the Q-multiplier in 1952. The circuit was originally described in Electronics and then was picked up and promoted by CQ. It was briefly popular because it was inexpensive and could be added outboard to existing receivers with inadequate selectivity. It shared the faults of very high Q, single circuits with the crystal filter - a sharp peak and poor skirts.

Another significant new feature of receivers during the 1946-55 decade was the use of multiple conversions to provide a high IF for superior image rejection and a low IF for selectivity. All the manufacturers, except Collins, retained the tuned HFO along with a crystal controlled second oscillator. Thus, by adding a converter to the signal path they were able to achieve double conversion yet retain, basically, the familiar, comfortable straight superheterodyne.

The first Hallicrafters double conversion receiver was the SX-71 in 1950. This receiver also departed drastically from the traditional Hallicrafters appearance with its two slide-rule dials. The SX-71 had intermediate frequencies of 2075 and 455 kHz with the standard single crystal filter in the 455 kHz IF.

In the same year Hammarlund delivered their new SP-600 with IF's of 3955 and 455 kHz. And in 1952 National joined the bandwagon with the HRO-60 (2010 and 456 kHz) and the NC-183D (1720 and 455 kHz). All of these receivers also used Lamb's crystal filter in the second IF.

The Hammarlund SP-600 was perhaps the ultimate refinement of the straight superheterodyne with a tunable HFO. The "Series 600 Super-Pro" was announced with a full page display in the 1948 ARRL Handbook. It was finally delivered about 1950 with a considerably different appearance and tube lineup than that shown in the Handbook advertisement. The set featured a rotating coil turret and one of the smoothest tuning mechanisms ever built.

The September, 1953, issue of Radio & Television News shows a picture of the 10,000th SP-600 coming off the production line. Since the SP-600 was being sold as late as 1972 it must have been one of the highest production receivers ever.

National continued to produce their classic HRO during the decade. The first postwar model, the HRO-5, was little changed from the original. It was replaced in 1947 with the HRO-7 with a streamlined cabinet but no basic changes in circuitry. In a drastically redesigned receiver, the HRO-50, in 1951, the power supply was brought into the cabinet, tubes changed to miniature types and a direct reading, slide-rule dial added. The HRO-50-1 added an IF stage and cascaded the IF transformers in 1951. The final model, the HRO-60, was introduced in 1952 and remained in production until 1964. The HRO-60 included double conversion but retained the original ganged plug-in coils and PW dial.

Seven page advertisements in the December, 1953, CQ and the January, 1954, QST heralded the most lavishly promoted receiver ever, the Hallicrafters SX-88. An impressive 20 tube receiver, it introduced a successful styling and electrical concept that Hallicrafters used for many years. Electrically the SX-88 was a two dial, double conversion receiver with a first IF of 2075 kHz and employing the 50 kHz second IF introduced in 1951 with the S-76. In spite of the massive advertising which accompanied its debut the SX-88 was not a success and it was last advertised in November, 1954, only eleven months after its introduction. However, the SX-88's basic design and styling lived on in the popular SX-100 and several other models.

Another beneficiary of a high-powered advertising campaign was National's "dream receiver," the NC-300. The unveiling of the receiver on September, 30, 1955, was preceded by an eight month campaign of "dream receiver" design contests and by advertisements showing a receiver covered with a tarpaulin, ready for unveiling, like a new work of sculpture. The NC-300 covered only the amateur bands with a first IF of 2215 kHz and a second IF of 80 kHz, a high C HFO and large slide-rule dial.

THE END IN SIGHT - 1956-65
THE SECOND POSTWAR DECADE

All the major communications receiver manufacturers were deep in trouble during the second postwar decade, 1956-65. RME, after over ten years of struggling disappeared in 1962. The 1950's were troubled years for Hallicrafters. Bill Halligan sold the company, repurchased it, and finally sold out to Northrop in the mid-1960's. Hammarlund hung on until 1967 when they were purchased by the first of a series of owners who used the Hammarlund name until it faded away in the 1970's. National struggled and declined during this same period. It survives today, a small operation doing military replacement business, in Chapter 11.

Collins lasted longer than the others because they were leaders and correctly judged the future shape of communications equipment. Today Collins is part of Rockwell International and still manufactures commercial and military communications receivers.

The heavy and cumbersome equipment of previous decades went out of style in the mid-1950's. Previously, weight and mass were de rigueur in a stable, quality receiver. A ham took pride in impressing visitors with a six foot rack of transmitting equipment and a table groaning under the load of a monster receiver.

Suddenly, desires changed. People wanted the new shoebox sized equipment. They wanted it to perform better, be more reliable and be more attractive by contemporary standards. Collins and Drake, a new company, guessed right and managed to prosper a little longer.

National and Hallicrafters were caught going the wrong way with bigger and heavier receivers. In 1955 National promoted the NC-300 as "Massive in the Modern Manner." In 1956 Hallicrafters advertisements said of the SX-101, which weighed 70 pounds and measured 20"X10½"X16", ". . .built like a battleship. Bigger. Heavier." Unfortunately, the public wanted their receivers to be less massive, smaller and lighter.

So, in 1957, as the old-line manufacturers made bigger and heavier receivers, Collins introduced the KWM-1, a complete 175 watt SSB transmitter and receiver, less power supply, in a package 6¼"X14"X 10" and weighing 15 pounds! Byron Goodman reviewed the KWM-1 in QST in 1958 and said, ". . .the KWM-1 may well mark the end of one era and the beginning of another. . .it could well be a way of life."

A newcomer, R. L. Drake, produced the first small, modern communications receiver, also in 1957. Their 1A was designed specifically for SSB and had many of the features of the Collins 75A at an economical price($299 vs $645). The 1A had a fixed HFO and a VFO feeding the second mixer. It had a bandpass first IF (2.9-3.5 mHz) rather than the tunable first IF of the 75A. A third IF of 50 kHz provide selectivity. The 1A was the ancestor of a long line of Drake receivers which culminated with the last receiver to use vacuum tubes, the R-4C which was sold until 1980.

Collins continued to push the new, small concept in 1958 when they replaced the 75A series with the 75S-1 receiver. They introduced their new "S" line of ham equipment in November, 1958, with four page, full color advertisements. The 75S-1 was not dramatically new electrically, most of its features having appeared previously in the KWM-1 and Drake 1A. But its new long and low appearance can still be recognized in most receivers and transceivers to this day.

As Goodman foresaw, the trend to transceivers eventually almost eliminated the separate communications receiver. The trend started slowly with Collins alone for a number of years. One reason was that the "S" line successor to the KWM-1, the KWM-2, cost $1150. Swan Engineering, another new company, eliminated the cost factor with a line of single band transceivers selling for $275 in 1961. Within a few years a dozen companies offered transceivers.

While reeling from the change in public taste to compact, light equipment and the trend to transceivers the communications receiver companies had another problem looming. The solid-state revolution was gaining on them and they didn't know what to do about it.

There was a popular notion that tubes were and always would be superior performers in the signal paths of receivers which made it easier for manufacturers to rationalize that they could continue with the old, familiar ways.

But the military was already going full speed into solid state. In 1956 Regency made news with the ATC-1 transistorized amateur band converter. In January, 1962, Davco announced the DR-30 all solid-state receiver. This receiver, using the Collins conversion system as used in the 75S-1 and Drake 1A, was a comparative miniature at 7½"X5"X4" and weighing seven pounds. In December, 1962, Faust Gonset announced the formation of Sideband Engineers and the availability of the SBE-33 transceiver which was completely solid-state except for the driver and final. It measured only 5½"X11½"X10½" and weighed 15 pounds including the power supply.

Perhaps the end for the vacuum tube communications receiver came in October, 1964. It was in that month, exactly 30 years after the introduction of the original HRO, that National announced the HRO-500. It was the first solid-state, high performance, general coverage communications receiver. The HRO-500 immediately became the ultimate receiver. Unfortuna-

tely, it did not save National. Nor did the belated solid-state efforts of the other manufacturers save them. The Japanese were in the wings.

The vacuum tube communications receiver lasted less than 50 years. The last one to be manufactured was the Drake R-4C which was discontinued in 1980. It was a hybrid receiver using six tubes along with 39 semiconductors.

SECTION II

THE TABLES

<u>NOTE:</u> Where the "<u>TYPE:</u>" of receiver is not listed it is a straight, signle conversion Superheterodyne.

<u>ALLIED (KNIGHT)</u>

Allied was a large mail order distributor located in Chicago. They issued annual catalogs of radio and electronic equipment and components from the 1930's through 1970 when they were acquired by Radio Shack. The name disappeared within a few years. They sold housebrand equipment under both the Allied and Knight names.

<u>MODEL:</u> A-2516 <u>YRS:</u> 1970 <u>PRICE:</u> $170 <u>BANDS:</u> 8 600 kHz bands, 80-10 ham bands + WWV <u>TYPE:</u> Dual conversion, fixed HFO <u>IF:</u> 8900-9500, 455 kHz <u>FILTER:</u> Crystal lattice <u>TUBES:</u> 7 + 6 diodes + 2 transistors 6BZ6 rf, 6BL8 mix1/xco, 6BE6 mix2, 2SC185 vfo, 2SC185 vfo buff, 2 6BA6 if, 6AQ8 prod det/bfo, 6BM8 af1/af out, CR1, CR4 agc, CR2 det, CR3 anl, CR5 vr, CR6 rect <u>REMARKS:</u> Probably made in Japan.

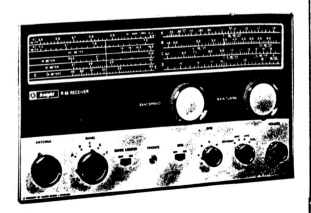

<u>ALLIED (KNIGHT)</u>

<u>MODEL:</u> R-55 <u>YRS:</u> 1960-61 <u>PRICE:</u> $67.50 <u>BANDS:</u> 5, .53-36, 47-56 mHz <u>IF:</u> 1650 kHz <u>FILTER:</u> None <u>TUBES:</u> 6, 6BE6 conv, 6DK6 if1, 6AW8 if2/af1, 6AL5 det/nl, 6AW8 af out/bfo, EZ90(6X4) rect <u>REMARKS:</u> Internal speaker, kit.

<u>MODEL:</u> R-100 <u>YRS:</u> 1959-61 <u>PRICE:</u> $104.50 <u>BANDS:</u> 4, .54-30 mHz <u>IF:</u> 455 kHz <u>FILTER:</u> Q-multiplier <u>TUBES:</u> 9, 6BZ6 rf, 6BH6 mix/ hfo, 6AZ8 if1, 6AZ8 if2/af1, ECC83(12AX7) q mult, 6BC7 avc/det/anl, 6AW8 af out/ bfo, 0B2 vr, 6X4 rect <u>REMARKS:</u> Kit, stock no. Y-726.

<u>MODEL:</u> R-100A <u>YRS:</u> 1962-63 <u>PRICE:</u> $99.95 <u>BANDS:</u> 4, .54-30 mHz <u>IF:</u> 455 kHz <u>FILTER:</u> Q-multiplier <u>TUBES:</u> 9, 6BZ6 rf, 6BH8 mix/hfo, 6AZ8 if1, 6AZ8 if2/af1,6BC7 det/avc/nl, 12AX7 q mult, 6AW8 af out/ bfo, 0B2 vr, 6X4 rect <u>REMARKS:</u> Kit, optional "S" meter and calibrator.

<u>MODEL:</u> Y-726 <u>YRS:</u> 1958-59 <u>PRICE:</u> $104.50 <u>BANDS:</u> 4, .54-30 mHz <u>IF:</u> 455 kHz <u>FILTER:</u> Q-multiplier <u>TUBES:</u> 8, 6BZ6 rf, 6BH8 conv 6AZ8 if1/af1, 6AZ8 if2/mtr amp, 6BC7 avc/ det/anl, 12AX7 q mult, 6AW8 af out/bfo, rect <u>REMARKS:</u> Kit.

<u>AUTOMATION ELECTRONICS</u>

See Pierson-Holt.

BARRETT

The Barrett Mfg Co, 1382 16th Avenue, San Francisco, CA, had a brief fling at making communications receivers in 1934.

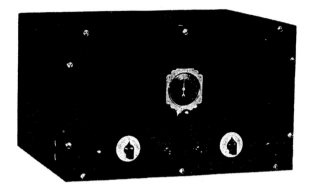

MODEL: DX-8 YRS: 1934 PRICE: $72.50
BANDS: 5, 1.5-30 mHz IF: 525 kHz FILTER: Crystal TUBES: 8 REMARKS: Plug-in coils.

BOULEVARD ELECTRONICS

Boulevard Electronics, Inc, 808-10 W. Jackson Blvd, Chicago, a distributor, advertised a communications receiver kit in 1953.

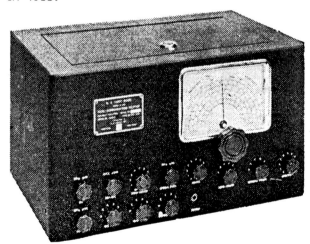

MODEL: None YRS: 1953 PRICE: $69.50
BANDS: 6, 0.2-0.4, .49-19 mHz IF: 455 kHz
FILTER: Crystal TUBES: 11 + sel rect, 6SG7 rf, 6SB7 conv, 2 6SG7 if, 6H6 det/nl, 6SF7 avc amp, 6SL7 bfo/af1, 6SL7 ph inv, 2 25L6 p/p af out, VR-75 vr, sel rect AF OUT: 2 W. REMARKS: Kit, 105-125 V., AC/DC

BRETING

The Breting Radio Manufacturing Co, 1815 Venice Blvd, Los Angeles, produced

communications receivers from 1934 to 1940. Ray Gudie, who had previously designed the PR-10 for Patterson (q.v.), was their chief engineer. The listed address was actually that of Gilfillan Bros who manufactured the chassis not only for Breting but for Patterson, Pierson-DeLane and scores of other companies because they had the necessary RCA licenses.

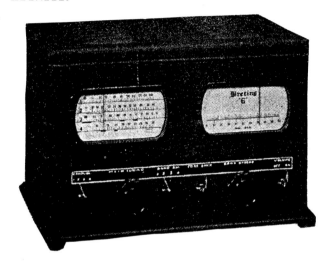

MODEL: 6 YRS: 1939-40 PRICE: $32.40
BANDS: 4, .55-30 mHz TUBES: 6 REMARKS: Internal speaker.

MODEL: 9 YRS: 1938-40 PRICE: $54 BANDS: 4, .54-34 mHz TUBES: 9 AF OUT: 3 W.

BRETING

MODEL: 12 YRS: 1935-36 PRICE: $93 BANDS: .55-30 mHz FILTER: Crystal TUBES: 12, 6B7 rf1/mtr amp, 6D6 rf2, 6C6 mix, 6D6 hfo, 2 6D6 if, 6B7 det/avc/af1, 42 af2, 6D6 bfo, 2 42 p/p af out, 5Z3 rect REMARKS: Dual meters read percent modulation and field strength.

MODEL: 14 YRS: 1936 PRICE: $99 BANDS: 5, .55-34 mHz FILTER: Crystal TUBES: 14

MODEL: 14AX YRS: 1938 PRICE: $99

MODEL: 40 YRS: 1939-40 PRICE: $99 BANDS: 5, .55-34 mHz FILTER: Crystal TUBES: 14 AF OUT: 18 W.

BRETING

MODEL: 49 YRS: 1938-39 PRICE: $99 BANDS: 4, .55-34 mHz IF: 1560 kHz TUBES: 13, including 1852 rf.

CARDWELL

The Allen D. Cardwell Manufacturing Co., Plainville, Conn., was a major component manufacturer, particularly noted for fixed capacitors. After the war they had a brief fling at receiver manufacturing.

MODEL: CR-54 YRS: 1946-47 BANDS: 6, .54-40 mHz FILTER: Crystal TUBES: 18 AF OUT: 8 W. REMARKS: Turret band switching, optional coverage to 54 mHz.

CENTRAL ELECTRONICS

Central Electronics in Chicago announced in their advertisements in mid-1959, "coming up! A new companion receiver which will transceive with the 100V transmitter." As far as is known, this receiver was never produced or sold.

COLLINS

Arthur Collins started manufacturing amateur transmitters in the basement of his house in Cedar Rapids, Iowa, in 1931. By 1933 the business had grown enough that the Collins Radio Co. had to move to leased facilities in downtown Cedar Rapids. Collins transmitters were used by the Byrd Antarctic expedition in 1933 and the

COLLINS

COLLINS

the resulting publicity enabled the little company to grow rapidly in the depression days of the 1930's.

The quality design and construction of the Collins equipment soon attracted the attention of broadcast, commercial and government users and the business expanded beyond the amateur market. By the end of the decade Collins was a major supplier of transmitters to the commercial airlines.

Employment at Collins Radio had grown to 150 by 1940. During World War II the company produced transmitters for the armed services. Collins turned out 26,000 of the 100 W. AN/ART-13 airborne transmitters during those years and, incidentally, other companies produced another 90,000 of the Collins designed equipment. The company also manufactured 35,000 of the TCS vehicular transmitter-receiver. At the wartime peak in 1945 Collins' employment reached 3332.

The amateur equipment part of Collins' business began to decline almost from the start and by the post-war years it was only a minor part of their output. However, they were best known to the public for their quality amateur transmitters and receivers and the amateur division remained important to the company for public relations purposes until very recently.

Collins came out with the 75A receiver in 1946. This was the first departure from the original straight superheterodyne with tunable HFO which had been the standard since the Hammarlund Comet in 1931. The 75A used a fixed, crystal controlled first oscillator with a permeability tuned second oscillator to set a new standard for frequency stability and readout accuracy.

The 75A covered only the ham bands and developed into the 75A-1 (1947), 75A-2 (1950), 75A-3 (1952) and 75A-4 (1955). The 75A-4 is considered an all-time classic amateur receiver.

The 51J series of general coverage receivers also developed from the 75A and was similar electrically and mechanically to the 75A. The series included the 51J-1 (1949), 51J-2, 51J-3 and 51J-4 (1955) as well as the military R-381 and R-388. The design finally evolved into the mechanically marvelous military receiver, the R-390 and R-390A. These massive digital readout sets were perhaps the ultimate vacuum tube receivers.

In 1958 Collins replaced the 75A series with the smaller and lighter "S" line. The amateur band sets were the 75S-1 (1958), 75S-2, 75S-3 (1961) and the 75S-3B which retained the basic 75A conversion system. The general coverage "S" line receiver was the 51S-1 which was manufactured from 1959 to 1972.

By the late 1960's Collins had grown to a $500 million company but, like many defense contractors, was having financial problems. Collins Radio was acquired by Rockwell International in 1971. Arthur Collins stayed on briefly after the merger but resigned in 1972 and formed a consulting firm in Dallas. He died in 1987.

The Collins Radio division of Rockwell still manufactures military and commercial solid-state communications receivers.

MODEL: 51F YRS: 1940 BANDS: 1 fixed frequency, 1.5-20 mHz TUBES: 11 AF OUT: 0.5 W. REMARKS: Fixed frequency receiver.

MODEL: 51-H YRS: 1945-52 REMARKS: AN/ARR-15

MODEL: 51J-1 YRS: 1949 PRICE: $875
BANDS: 30, 0.5-30.5 mHz FILTER; Crystal

MODEL: 51J-2 YRS: 1949

MODEL: 51J-3 YRS: 1950-51 BANDS: 30,
0.5-30 mHz TYPE: Dual conversion, fixed
hfo IF: 2500-1500(2500-3500), 500 kHz
FILTER: Xtal TUBES: 18 + diode, 6AK5 rf,
6BE6 mix1, 6AK5 xco, 6BE6 band 1 mix,
6BE6 band 2 mix, 6BA6 vfo, 6BA6 buff,
3 6BA6 if, 12AX7 det/avc rect, 6BA6 bfo,
12AU7 if k fol/avc amp, 12AX7 nl/af1,
6AQ5 af out, 6BA6 calib, 0A2 vr, 5V4
rect, meter amp AF OUT: 2.5 W.

MODEL: 51J-4 YRS: 1952-62 PRICE: $1099
BANDS: 30, .54-30.5 mHz TYPE: Double conversion, fixed hfo IF: 3500-2500(2500-
1500), 500 kHz FILTER: Xtal and mechanical TUBES: 19 + diode, 6AK5 rf, 6BE6 mix1,
6BA6 xco, 6BE6 band 1 mix, 6BE6 mix2,
6BA6 vfo, 6BA6 vfo buff, 4 6BA6 if, 12AU7
if k fol/avc amp, 6BA6 bfo, 12AX7 avc
rect/det, 12AX7 nl/af1, 6AQ5 af out,
6BA6 calib, 0A2 vr, 5V4 rect, CR101 meter
rect AF OUT: 2.5 W.

MODEL: 51J-5 Prototype REMARKS: Prototype model, only one made.

MODEL: 51J-6 YRS: 1957 BANDS: 31, 0.2-
31 mHz REMARKS: Shown in 1958 Collins
catalog. Looks like prototype of 51S-1.
Probably never manufactured. Q-multiplier and product detector.

MODEL: 51-Q YRS: 1940-44 BANDS: 4, 1.5-
12 mHz TUBES: 7, 3 12SK7, 2 12A6, 12SQ7,
12SA7 REMARKS: Operates on 12 VDC.

MODEL: 51S-1 YRS: 1959-72 PRICE: $1828
BANDS: 30, 0.2-30 mHz TYPE: Double conversion, fixed HFO IF: 3000-2000, 500 kHz
FILTER: Mechanical TUBES: 17 + 1 trans +
17 diodes, 6DC6 rf, 6U8A mix1/xco, 6U8A
mix 2/xco, 6U8A mix3/rem cont gate,
6136 vfo, 3 6BA6 if, 12AX7 q mult, 6BA6
agc amp, 5670 if k fol/agc k fol, 12AX7
line af1/local af1, 6BF5 local af 2, 6AK6

COLLINS

line af2, 6BA6 bfo, 4 1N128 prod det, CR5 mtr rect, 8 1N1695 rect, 1N482A agc rect, 1N128 am det, 1N482A agc stabil, 1N67A muting trans supr, 2N647 ssb/cw af amp AF OUT: 1 W REMARKS: 8500 built.

MODEL: 51S-1 Variations REMARKS: Changes in some production runs: 6EA8 replaced 6U8A, 7543 replaced 6136 vfo, 7543 replaced 6BA6 bfo, 2N388 or 2N2222A replaced 2N647 ssb/cw af amp, added 2 zener diodes to vfo, added 4 diodes for meter bridge rect.

MODEL: 51S-1A TUBES: 17 + 5 trans + 15 diodes, same lineup as 51S-1 except 3 1N1492 DC power supply rectifiers, 4 2N637B DC power supply switching transistors which replace 8 1N1696 REMARKS: 51S-1 with 28 VDC power supply.

MODEL: 51S-1AF REMARKS: Rack mounted 51S-1A.

MODEL: 51S-1B REMARKS: 51S-1 with rear mounted junction box with military-type connectors for power, control, audio and antenna lines.

MODEL: 51S-1F REMARKS: Rack mounted version of 51S-1.

MODEL: 75A YRS: 1946-47 BANDS: 6 ham bands, 80-10 mtrs TYPE: Double conversion, fixed hfo FILTER: Xtal TUBES: 14

COLLINS

MODEL: 75A-1 YRS: 1947-49 PRICE: $375 BANDS: 6 ham bands, 80-10 mtrs TYPE: Double conversion, fixed HFO IF: 1500-2500 (3500-5500, 500 kHz FILTER: Crystal TUBES: 14, 6AK5 rf, 6SA7 mix1, 6AK5 xco, 6SK7 if1, 6L7 mix2, 6SJ7 vfo, 2 6SG7 if, 6SJ7 avc, 6H6 det/nl, 6SJ7 bfo, 6SJ7 af1, 6V6 af out, 5Y3 rect REMARKS: Differs from 75A in limiter switch on right above function knob.

MODEL: 75A-2 YRS: 1950-52 PRICE: $420 BANDS: 7 ham bands, 160-10 mtrs TYPE: Double conversion, fixed HFO IF: 2500-1500(5455-3455), 455 kHz FILTER: Crystal TUBES: 16, 6AK5 rf, 6BE6 mix1, 12AT7 xco, 6BE6 mix2, 6BA6 vfo, 6BA6 vfo buff, 3 6BA6 if, 6AL5 avc/det, 6BA6 bfo, 6AL5 nl, 12AX7 avc amp/af1, 6AL5 cw nl, 6AQ5 af out, 5Y3 rect AF OUT: 2.5 W.

MODEL: 75A-2 (Variation) TUBES: 17, adds an 0A2 to original 75A-2 complement.

MODEL: 75A2A YRS: 1953 FILTER: Crystal and mechanical REMARKS: 75A-2 converted to 75A-3 by addition of mechanical filter.

MODEL: 75A-3 YRS: 1953-54 PRICE: $530
BANDS: 7 ham bands, 160-10 mtrs TYPE:
Double conversion, fixed hfo IF: 2500-
1500(5455-3455), 455 kHz FILTER: Xtal and
mechanical TUBES: 18, 6CB6 rf, 6BA7
mix1, 12AT7 xco, 6BA7 mix2, 6BA6 vfo,
6BA6 vfo buff, 4 6BA6 if, 6AL5 det/avc
rect, 12AX7 avc amp/af1, 6AL5 anl,
6BA6 bfo, 6AL5 cw nl, 6AQ5 af out,
0A2 vr, 5Y3 rect AF OUT: 2.5 W.

MODEL: 75A4 YRS: 1955-58 PRICE: $645
BANDS: 7 1 mHz ham bands, 10-160 mtrs
TYPE: Double conversion, fixed hfo
IF: 1500-2500, 455 kHz FILTER: Mechanical TUBES: 22, 6DC6 rf, 6BA7 mix1,
12AT7 xco, 6BA7 mix2, 6BA6 vfo, 6
BA6 vfo buff, 6BA6 if, 12AT7 Q Mult,
6BA6 if2, 6BA6 if3, 6AL5 det, 12AU7 prod
det, 6BA6 bfo, 6BA6 avc amp, 6AL5 avc/
noise clip, 6AL5 gain gate/bias rect,
12AT7 af1, 6AQ5 af out, 6AL5 nl, 6BA6
calib, 0A2 vr, 5Y3 rect AF OUT: 0.75 W.

MODEL: 75A-4 (Variation) YRS: 1957-58 REM-
ARKS: Latest production version of 75A-4,
"prized by 75A-4 connoisseurs." Serial
numbers from 4200 and up, has vernier
tuning knob and is identified by labelling
for NOISE LIMITER/AM CS-SSB on the same
horizontal line in the upper right corner.

MODEL: 75S-1 YRS: 1958-61 PRICE: $495
BANDS: 14 200 kHz bands 3.4-30 mHz
TYPE: Double conversion, fixed hfo
IF: 2955-3155, 455 kHz FILTER: Mechanical TUBES: 10 + 4 semi diodes, 6DC6 rf,
6U8A mix/xco, 6U8A mix2/k fol, 6AU6 vfo,
2 6BA6 if, 6AT6 avc/det/af1, 6U8A prod
det/bfo, 6BF5 af out, 1N34 freq shift
sw, 2 1N1084 rect, sel rect.

MODEL: 75S-2 PRICE: $600 REMARKS:
75S-1 with 14 additional 200 kHz bands.

COLLINS

MODEL: 75S-3 YRS: 1961-63 PRICE: $620
BANDS: 14 200 kHz bands 3.4-30 mHz
TYPE: Double conversion, fixed hfo.
IF: 2955-3155, 455 kHz FILTER: Mechanical
TUBES: 12 + 6 semi diodes, 6DC6 rf,
6U8A mix1/xco, 6U8A mix2/k fol, 6AU6
vfo, 12AX7 q mult, 2 6BA6 if, 6U8A prod
det/bfo, 6AT6 det/avc/af1, 6DC6 var bfo
6DC6 xtal cal, 6BF5 af out, 2 1N1084
rect, sel rect, HC7004 bfo tune, 1N732
vr, 1N34A switch REMARKS: Differs from
75S-1: adds reject tuning, variable or
xtal bfo, concentric rf/af gain, agc
selector.

MODEL: 75S-3 (Variation) REMARKS:
Replaces 2 1N1084 and sel rect with 3
1N1490.

MODEL: 75S-3A PRICE: $750 REMARKS:
75S3 with 14 additional 200 kHz bands.

MODEL: 75S-3B YRS: 1964-76 PRICE: $620
BANDS: 14 200 kHz bands 3.4-30 mHz
TYPE: Double conversion, fixed hfo
IF: 2955-3155, 455 kHz FILTER: Mechanical TUBES: 12 + 7 semi diodes, 6DC6 rf,
6EA8 mix1/xco, 6EA8 mix2/k fol, 6AU6
vfo, 12AX7 q mult, 2 6BA6 if, 6AT6 det/
avc/af1, 6EA8 prod det/xtal bfo, 6DC6
var bfo, 6DC6 xtal cal, 6BF5 af out,

COLLINS

3 1N1492 (or 1N1096) rect, HC7004 bfo
tune, 1N732A vr, 1N3010A vr, 1N34A
switch AF OUT: 3 W. REMARKS: Changes
from previous model: furnished with one
if filter (SSB) plus 2 positions for optional cw filters, new 3 W. af output,
oscillator zener regulated, am filter
socket.

MODEL: 75S-3B (Variation) REMARKS: Later versions have 7543 vfo, replacing
6AU6.

MODEL: 75S-3C PRICE: $850 REMARKS:
75S-3B with 14 additional 200 kHz bands.

Courtesy AWA and *Old Timers Bulletin*.

MODEL: COL-46159 YRS: 1940-44 BANDS:
3, 1.5-12 mHz IF: 455 kHz FILTER: None
TUBES: 7, 12SK7 rf, 12SA7 mix, 12A6 hfo,
2 12SK& if, 12SQ7 det/af1/bfo, 12A6 af out
REMARKS: Part of TCS set built for U S
Navy. Also designated 51-Q (qv).

MODEL: R-381/URR-23 REMARKS: 51J-2

COLLINS

COLLINS

MODEL: R-388 REMARKS: Military 51J-3

MODEL: R-388A REMARKS: R388 with mechanical filters and nonmagnetic side panels made for U S Navy.

MODEL: R-390 YRS: 1950-54 BANDS: 32 1 mHz bands, 0.5-32 mHz TYPE: Double conversion, fixed HFO from 8-32 mHz, triple conversion 0.5-8 mHz IF: 9-18 mHz (0.5-8 mHz only), 3000-2000, 455 kHz FILTER: Crystal + 455 kHz cascaded L/C TUBES: 32 + 1 semi diode, 6AJ5 rf1, 6BJ6 rf2, 6C4 mix1, 6AJ5 xco, 6C4 mix2, 6AJ5 xco, 6C4 mix3, 5749 vfo, 5 6BJ6 if, 6AK6 if, 12AU7 det/nl, 5749 bfo, 12AU7 af1/sq, 12AU7 nl/agc rect, 12AU7 loc af1/line af1, 6AK6 loc af out, 6AK6 line af out, 6BJ6 agc amp, 12AU7 if k fol/agc time const, 12AU7 calib/buff, 12AU7 multivib, 2 26Z5 rect, 2 6082 vr, 2 5652 vr, 6BH6 DC amp, si rect

MODEL: R-390A YRS: 1958- PRICE: $1421 BANDS: 32, 0.5-32 mHz TYPE: Double/ triple conversion, fixed hfo IF: 17.5-25 mHz(0.5-8 mHz only), 2.5-2 mHz(0.5-1 mHz band only), 3-2 mHz, 455 kHz FILTER: Crystal and mechanical TUBES: 24, 6DC6 rf, 6C4 mix1, 6AK5W xco, 6C4 mix2, 6AK5W xco, 6C4 mix3, 6BA6W vfo, 3 6BA6W if, 5814A det/agc time, 5814A k fol, agc rect, 6BA6W agc amp, 5814A af1/ k fol, 5814A af2 line/af2 local, 6AK6 af out local, 6AK6 af out line, 6BA6W bfo, 2 26Z5W rect, 0A2 vr, 5814A calib/k fol, 5814A multivib, 5814A lim AF OUT: 0.5 W.

REMARKS: Developed and designed by Collins as reduced cost R-390. Only 525 Manufactured by Collins, thousands more by Motorola, Electronic Assistance Corp, and Stewart Warner, often using Collins components (VFO's, etc).

MODEL: R-391 REMARKS: R-390 with remote tuning for seven channels.

MODEL: R-391A REMARKS: R-390A with remote tuning for seven channels.

Courtesy Electric Radio

MODEL: R-392 YRS: 1950-1960 BANDS: 32, 0.5-32 mHz TYPE: Double/triple conversion, fixed HFO IF: 9.5-18 mHz (0.5-8 mHz only), 2-3 mHz, 455 kHz FILTER: 455 kHz L/C TUBES: Includes 2 rf and 6 if stages REMARKS: Compact, ruggedized R-390. Operates from 28 VDC. Part of GRC-19. Also manufactured by Stewart Warner, Western Electric and others.

DRAKE

The R L Drake Company of Miamisburg, OH, was founded in 1943 by Robert Lloyd Drake in Dayton and originally manufactured high-pass and low-pass RF filters for the ham and military markets. They moved to Miamisburg in 1953 and added a number of small ham accessories to their product line.

Drake entered the receiver business in 1957 with the novel 1-A. The 1-A was the first of the small, modern communications receivers geared to SSB and set the future course for receivers at a time when National and Hallicrafters were still committed to their massive receivers of the past.

The 1-A was followed by the 2- series and, later, by the classic R-4 series which Drake manufactured until 1980. The company abandoned the ham business in the early 1980's in favor of home satellite receivers. However, they have recently announced an advanced solid-state receiver for 1991.

R L Drake died in 1975 and Peter W. Drake assumed leadership of the company.

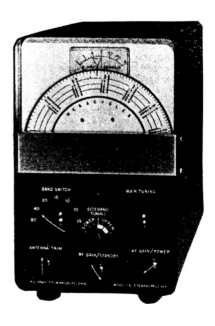

MODEL: 1-A YRS: 1957-58 PRICE: $299 TYPE: Triple conversion, fixed hfo BANDS: 7 600 kHz ham bands, 10-80 mtrs IF: 2900-3500, 1100, 50 kHz FILTER: 50 kHz L/C TUBES:

DRAKE

DRAKE

11, 6DC6 rf, 6BY6 mix1, 6AB4 xco, 6BY6 mix2, 6BQ7A vfo/k fol, 6BY6 conv, 12AU7 prod det, 6BF6 avc amp/rect, 12AU7 af1/bfo, 12AQ5 af out, 12X4 rect

MODEL: 1-A (Variation) YRS: 1958-59 PRICE: $299 BANDS: 7 600 kHz ham bands (plus WWV), 10-80 mtrs TYPE: Triple conversion, fixed hfo IF: 2900-3500, 1100, 50 kHz FILTER: 50 kHz L/C TUBES: 13, 6BZ6 rf, 6AB4 xco, 6BE6 mix1, 6BQ7A vfo, 6BE6 mix2, 6BY6 conv, 6BZ6 if, 6BJ8 avc amp/rect, 12BA6 calib, 12AU7 prod det, 12AU7 bfo/af1, 12AQ5 af out, 12X4 rect REMARKS: Internal speaker, adds crystal calibrator and switch, WWV position, additional IF tube.

MODEL: 2-A YRS: 1959-61 PRICE: $269.95 BANDS: 12 600 kHz bands 3.5-30 mHz

DRAKE

TYPE: Triple conversion, fixed hfo IF:
3500-4100, 455, 50 kHz FILTER: 50 kHz L/C
TUBES: 10 + Ge rect, 6BZ6 rf, 6U8 mix1/xco,
6BE6 mix2/vfo, 6BE6 mix3/xco, 6BA6 if,
6BF6 det/avc, 6BE6 prod det/bfo, 6AV6
af1, 1N34 bias rect, 6AQ5 af out, 6X4 rect
REMARKS: Separate preselector tuning.
Some sources show 6BZ6 if tube (vs
6BA6).

MODEL: 2-B YRS: 1961-65 PRICE: $279.95
BANDS: 12 600 kHz bands 3.5-30 mHz TYPE:
Triple conversion, fixed hfo IF: 3500-4100,
455, 50 kHz FILTER: 50 kHz L/C TUBES: 10,
6BZ6 rf, 6U8 mix1/xco, 6BE6 mix2/vfo,
6BE6 mix3/xco, 6BA6 if, 6BE6 prod det/bfo,
6BF6 det/avc, 6BN6 af1/bias rect/fil,
6AQ5 af out, 6X4 rect AF OUT: 1 W.
REMARKS: New passband tuner, improved
selectivity.

MODEL: 2-C YEARS: 1966-73 PRICE: $229
BANDS: 5 500 kHz bands, 3-30 mHz TYPE:
Triple conversion, fixed HFO IF: 3500-

DRAKE

4000, 455, 50 kHz FILTER: 50 kHz L/C
TUBES: 5 + 3 semi diodes + 7 transistors,
12BZ6 rf, 12AU6 mix1, 2N3394 xco, 12BE6
mix2/vfo, 12BE6 mix3/xco, 12BA6 if, 1N270
det, 2N3394 af1, 2 1N270 prod det, 2N3394
bfo, 2 2N3394 af, 2N3394 avc amp, 40310
af out AF OUT: 1.8 W.

MODEL: R-4 YRS: 1964-66 PRICE: $379.95
BANDS: 15 500 kHz bands, 1.5-30 mHz TYPE:
Double conversion, pre-mixer IF: 5645,
50 kHz FILTER: 50 kHz L/C, xtal lattice
TUBES: 13 + 7 semi diodes, 12BZ6 rf,
12BZ6 calib, 6KZ8 mix1/k fol, 6AU6 pto,
2 12BA6 if, 6KZ8 premix/xco, 12BE6 mix2/
xco, 12AV6 avc amp/det, 6GX6 prod det/
af1, 12EH5 af out, 12BA6 nb amp, 12AX7
nb pulse amp/shaper, 1N625 nb gate,
2 1N625 nb pulse clip, 1N625 am det,
1N625 bias rect, 2 1N3756 rect AF OUT:
1.4 W.

MODEL: R-4A YRS: 1966-67 PRICE: $399.95
BANDS: 15 500 kHz bands 1.5-30 mHz TYPE:
Double conversion, pre-mixer IF: 5645, 50
kHz FILTER: 50 kHz L/C, xtal filter TUBES:
14 + 4 diodes, 12BZ6 rf, 6HS6 mix 1, 6AU6
vfo, 6KZ8 pre-mix/xco, 12BE6 mix2/xco,
2 12BA6 if, 6GX6 prod det/af1, 12AV6 avc,
6EH5 af out, 0B2 vr, 12BA6 calib, 12BA6

DRAKE

noise blank, 12AX7 noise blank, 1N625
noise blank/det, ED-3004 bias rect, 2
1N3756 rect <u>AF OUT</u>: 1.4 W.

<u>MODEL</u>: R-4B <u>YRS</u>: 1968-73 <u>PRICE</u>: $430
<u>BANDS</u>: 15 500 kHz bands 1.5-30 mHz <u>TYPE</u>:
Double conversion, pre-mixer <u>IF</u>: 5645,
50 kHz <u>FILTER</u>: 50 kHz L/C, xtal lattice
<u>TUBES</u>: 9 + 10 trans + 17 diodes + 2 ic,
<u>AF OUT</u>: 1.5 W.

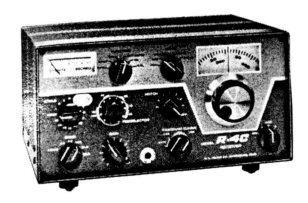

<u>MODEL</u>: R-4C <u>YRS</u>: 1973-80 <u>PRICE</u>: $499.65
<u>BANDS</u>: 20 500 kHz bands 1.5-30 mHz
<u>TYPE</u>: Double conversion, pre-mixer
<u>IF</u>: 5645, 50 kHz <u>FILTER</u>: Xtal lattice, 50
kHz L/C <u>TUBES</u>: 6 + 15 trans + 23 diodes
+ 1 ic, 6BA6 rf, 6EJ7 mix1, 6BE6 mix 2,
6EJ7 mix3, 6BA6 if, 6EJ7 premix, 2N5950
if1, EP487 power supply filter, 2N5950
source fol, 2N5953 xco, 2N3394 bfo,
2N3394 det/amp, 2N3877 agc, 2N5950 pto,
2N3394 af, 2N3394 af, 40310 af out,
2N3392 xco, 2N3563 pto buf, 2N5950 calib,
2N3394 calib shape, SN7473 calib div,
1N4148 agc, 2 1N270 prod det, 1N270 det,
1N270 premix clamp, 1N714 vr, 5 1N4005
rect, 2 1N4148 agc, 1N5240A vr, 1N4148

DRAKE

premix key, 1N270 calib shape, 1N714 vr,
2 1N4005 rect, 2 1N270 mix3 inj clip,
1N4148 agc, 1N4148 trans sup <u>AF OUT</u>: 2
W.

<u>MODEL</u>: SW-4A <u>YRS</u>: 1966-67 <u>PRICE</u>: $299.00
<u>BANDS</u>: 11 500 kHz bands, LW, MW, 49, 40,
31, 25, 19, 16, 15, 12 mtr SWBC <u>TYPE</u>:
Double conversion, pre-mixer <u>IF</u>: 5645,
455 kHz <u>FILTER</u>: Xtal lattice, 5645 kHz
<u>TUBES</u>: 6 + 7 trans + 8 diodes, 12BZ6 rf,
6HS6 mix1, 6HS6 premix, 12BE6 mix2,
2 12BA6 if, 2N706 vfo, 2N3894 vfo buff,
2N3858 agc amp, 2 2N3394 af1,2, 40310 af
out, 1N714 vr, 1N270 det, 1N483 avc clamp,
4 1N3194 rect, 1N3194 bias rect, 2N3394
premix xco <u>AF OUT</u>: 2 W <u>REMARKS</u>: International SWBC receiver.

ECHOPHONE

The Echophone Radio Co started in
the early 1920's in Southern California
where they owned radio stations and manufactured home broadcast receivers.
In 1930 they moved to Waukegan, IL, where
the company turned out 1000 sets per
day. They changed management in 1931
and later moved to 2611 Indiana Avenue
in Chicago. The depression and financial
difficulties hit Echophone in the mid
1930's and they finally suspended business in August, 1936.

Ray Durst, an Echophone executive,
got together with Bill Halligan, president of Hallicrafters, and they worked
out a deal where Hallicrafters acquired
the Indian Avenue plant and Echophone's
RCA manufacturing licenses. Hallicrafters moved their entire operation into

ECHOPHONE

the plant on August 15, 1936. Ray Durst became Hallicrafters vice president.

The Echophone name went into limbo until 1940 when Hallicrafters wanted to come out with a line of very low priced communications receivers. Rather than tarnish the Hallicrafters and Skyrider images they put the new sets out under the Echophone name. The sets were designed and produced in the Hallicrafters facility by Hallicrafters personnel.

MODEL: Echophone Commercial EC-1 YRS: 1940-44 PRICE: $19.95 ($24.50 1942) BANDS: 3 bands, .545-30 mHz FILTER: None TUBES: 6, 12K8 conv, 12SK7 if, 12LQ7 det/avc/af1, 12J5 bfo, 35L6 af out, 35Z5 rect REMARKS: AC/DC, internal speaker.

ECHOPHONE

MODEL: EC-1A YRS: 1945 PRICE: $29.50 BANDS: 3, .55-30 mHz FILTER: None TUBES: 6, 12SA7 conv, 12SK7 if, 12SQ7 det/avc/af1, 12SQ7 bfo/nl, 35L6 af out, 35Z5 rect REMARKS: AC/DC, internal speaker.

MODEL: EC-1B YRS: 1945 BANDS: 3, .55-30 mHz IF: 455 kHz FILTER: None TUBES: 6, 12SA7 conv, 12SK7 if, 12SQ7 det/avc/af1, 12SQ7 bfo, 35L6 af out, 35Z5 rect REMARKS: AC/DC, internal speaker. Eliminate noise limiter and phones/speaker switch.

MODEL: EC-2 YRS: 1941-43 PRICE: $29.95 BANDS: 3, .55-30 mHz FILTER: None IF: 455 kHz TUBES: 7 + ballast, 6SG7 rf, 6K8 conv, 6SK7 if, 6H6 det/avc/nl, 6SC7 bfo/af1, 25L6 af out, 25Z6 rect REMARKS: AC/DC, internal speaker.

ECHOPHONE

MODEL: EC-3 YRS: 1941-43 PRICE: $49.95
BANDS: 3, .545-30 mHz FILTER: crystal
TUBES: 10 REMARKS: AC/DC.

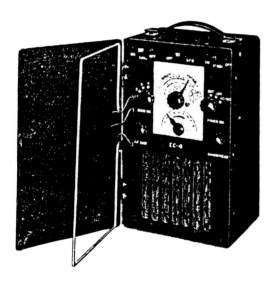

MODEL: EC-4 YRS: 1941-42 PRICE: $49.50
BANDS: 4, .545-32 mHz TUBES: 9 REMARKS:
Portable, 115 V. AC/DC, battery, internal
speaker, 2 loop antennas.

MODEL: EC-6 YRS: 1945 BANDS: 3, .55-
19 mHz FILTER: None TUBES: 7, 1R5 conv,
2 1N5 if, 1H5 det/avc/af1, 50L6 af out ac/
dc, 3Q5 af out battery, 35Z5 rect REM-
ARKS: AC/DC/battery portable BC receiver. Internal speaker. Same circuit as
Hallicrafters RE-1.

MODEL: EC-113 YRS: 1948 PRICE: $49.50
BANDS: 3, .54-22 mHz TUBES: 6 REMARKS:
AC/DC, per Dachis list.

EICO

EICO of New York sold kit type test instruments. They had one receiver
in their line for a brief time.

MODEL: 711 Space Ranger YRS: 1967 PRICE:
Kit $49.95, wired $69.95 BANDS: .55-30 mHz
REMARKS: Available kit or wired.

FEDERATED PURCHASER

Federated Purchaser, 25 Park Place,
NYC, offered a kit or assembled receiver
designed by Clifford Denton, their chief
engineer. Denton was a popular radio
writer of the 1930's.

MODEL: 30A Master Explorer TUBES:8 YRS:
1933

GENERAL MANUFACTURING

The General Manufacturing Co, Chicago, was a coil manufacturer. They put
out a kit receiver using their coils.

GENERAL MANUFACTURING

MODEL: Super DX-8 YRS: 1935 BANDS: 4,
1.6-18 mHz IF: 507 kHz FILTER: Crystal (Optional) TUBES: 8, 58 rf, 2A7 conv, 58 if,
2A6 det/avc/af1, 56 bfo, 56 af2, 2A5 af
out, 80 rect REMARKS: Kit with preassembled front-end unit.

GONSET

Faust Gonset formed the Gonset Co.,
of Burbank, CA, to manufacture ham
equipment during the 1950's. In the late
'50's they became a division of Young
Spring and Wire Corp. and soon disappeared. They were best known for VHF
transceivers.

MODEL: G-33 YRS: 1958-61 PRICE: $89.95
BANDS: 4, .54-34 mHz IF: 1650 kHz FILTER:
None TUBES: 6, 6BE6 conv, 6BA6 if1, 6BA6
if2/bfo, 6AV6 det/avc/af1, 6CM6 af out,
6X4 rect

MODEL: G-43 YRS: 1958-61 PRICE: $159.50
BANDS: 6, .54-30 mHz IF: 1650 kHz FILTER:
None TUBES: 8, 6BE6 conv, 2 6BA6 if, 6AU6
if3, 6AL5 det/avc/anl, 12AX7 af1/bfo, 6CM6
af out, 6X4 rect

GONSET

MODEL: G-63 YRS: 1959-61 PRICE: $239.50
BANDS: 6 ham bands, 80 - 6 mtrs TYPE:
Double conversion, variable hfo IF: 2085,
263 kHz FILTER: Q Multiplier TUBES: 11,
6BZ6 rf, 6U8A mix/hfo, 6BE6 conv, 2 6BA6
if, 6AL5 det/avc/anl, 6BE6 prod det/bfo,
12AX7 af1/q mult, 6AQ5 af out, OB2 vr,
5Y3 rect

MODEL: G-66 YRS: 1955-56 PRICE: $169.50
BANDS: 6, BC + 80-10 mtrs TYPE: Double
Conversion, variable hfo IF: 2050, 265 kHz
FILTER: None TUBES: 9, 6DC6 rf, 6U8 mix/
buf, 6C4 hfo, 6BE6 mix2/xco, 6AU6 if, 6AL5
det/avc/nl, 6AW8 af1/bfo, 6AQ5 af out,
OB2 vr AF OUT: 3 W. REMARKS: Separate
power supply.

GONSET

MODEL: G-66B YRS: 1957-59 PRICE: $189.50
BANDS: 6, BC + 80-10 mtrs TYPE: Double
conversion, tunable hfo IF: 2050, 262 kHz
FILTER: 8 262 kHz L/C circuits REMARKS:
Separate power supply. Distinguished by
emblem above "S" meter.

MODEL: GE43 YRS: 1961 PRICE: $99.50
BANDS: .54-30 mHz TUBES: 7

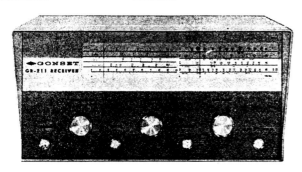

MODEL: GR-211 YRS: 1961-62 PRICE: $69.50
BANDS: 4, .54-34 mHz TUBES: 5 + 2 semi
rectifiers

MODEL: GR-212 YRS: 1961-62 PRICE: $99.50
BANDS: 6, .54-34 mHz TYPE: Double conversion, tunable hfo IF: 1650, 455 kHz FIL-
TER: None TUBES: 7 + 2 semi rect, 6U8
mix1/hfo, 6BA6 if1, 6BE6 mix2/xco, 6BA6
if2, 6AL5 det/avc/nl, 12AX7 af1/bfo, 6AQ5
af out, 2 semi rect

GUTHMAN

Edwin I. Guthman & Co., So. Peoria St.,
Chicago, Ill., hired the peripatetic McMurdo Silver as chief engineer after his latest company folded in 1938. Silver designed a line of ham equipment for Guthman
which included two receivers.

GUTHMAN

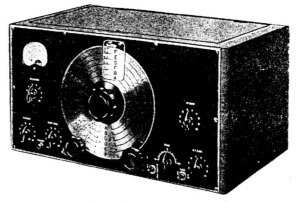

MODEL: U-17 Silver Super YRS: 1939
PRICE: $49.50 BANDS: 6, .54-61 mHz IF:
455 kHz FILTER: Regenerative if TUBES:
8, 6K8 conv, 7A7 if, 6B8 det/avc/af1/nl,
7A7 bfo, 7A7 mtr amp, 6V6 af out, VR150
vr, 80 rect AF OUT: 4.25 W. REMARKS:
Kit, regenerative mixer and IF amplifier.

MODEL: U-50K/W YRS: 1939-40 PRICE:
$57.45 assembled, $49.95 kit BANDS: 6,
.525-62 mHz IF: 455 kHz FILTER: Regenerative if TUBES: 11, 7A7, 6J5, 6SF5, 6K8,
VR105, 6B8, 2 6SK7, 2 7C5, 80 AF OUT: 12 W.
REMARKS: K = kit, W = wired.

HALLICRAFTERS

The most famous name in communications receivers, The Hallicrafters, Inc.,
was formed in September, 1933, and their
first advertisement for the H-13 all-wave
BC type receiver, appeared the same
month in Radio News under the Silver-
Marshall Mfg Co. name and address. A
short time later the Silver-Marshall Mfg
Co. issued their 1934 catalog devoted ex-

HALLICRAFTERS

clusively to the Hallicrafters line of home receivers. According to the catalog "Radio receivers bearing the Hallicrafters name will be the hand made product of an unfettered group of radio craftsmen."

William Halligan, a Bostonian who moved to Chicago in 1928, was an engineer who had a manufacturers rep business in the Chicago area. Business was not good in the early 1930's so he decided to get into manufacturing. Silver-Marshall Mfg Co. was a dummy corporation set up in 1929 solely to hold shares in Silver-Marshall Inc. When the latter went bankrupt in 1932 its stock became worthless leaving Silver-Marshall Mfg Co. with only its name as an asset. There was no equipment, no factory, no inventory. Halligan (Hallicrafters) acquired the right to use their name and corporate address. Kendall Clough, formerly chief engineer for Silver-Marshall Inc., joined him and designed the new line of receivers.

Their first communications receiver, the S-1 Skyrider, a five tube regenerative TRF, appeared in the 1934 Allied Radio catalog and the first advertisement was in the April, 1934, Radio News. In October, 1934, Hallicrafters announced their 1935 line consisting of the first Hallicrafters superheterodyne communications receiver, the seven tube Super-Skyrider which was similar to the later S-4 series, the five tube TRF and a "Deluxe All-Wave Superhet" BC type receiver.

Hallicrafters led a precarious existence during its early years. It did not have the vital RCA licenses and was constantly under financed. Late in 1934 they discontinued using the Silver-Marshall name and moved from the old Silver-Marshall address, 417 North State Street, to 3001 Southport Avenue, Chicago where they remained until early 1936. During this period they may have assembled a few receivers in spite of the lack of an RCA license but most of their sets were contracted out to Howard Radio. There is evidence that some sets were also made by RCA.

HALLICRAFTERS

Hallicrafters finally got their RCA licenses when Halligan formed a partnership with Arthur Case of another troubled company, Case Electric Co. of Marion, IN. Case Electric had the licenses and a good plant and Hallicrafters moved to Marion in April, 1936. However, the relationship did not work well and the company was still in financial difficulties when Bill Halligan got together with Ray Durst an executive with the foundering Echophone Radio Co. a couple of months later. Echophone had a large plant at 2611 Indiana Avenue, Chicago, and the RCA manufacturing licenses. They worked out a deal and Hallicrafters acquired the Echophone assets and four months after moving to Marion they moved back to Chicago on August 15, 1936. The company remained at 2611 Indiana Avenue until they built a new plant at 4401 West Fifth Avenue, Chicago, after World War II. Ray Durst became a Hallicrafters vice president and second in command.

Meanwhile, in 1935 developments in the receiver field came fast and Hallicrafters twice revamped its line during the year. Three new models of the Super Skyrider, the S-4, S-5 and S-6, differing in the frequuency ranges covered, were introduced in January. An optional crystal filter added an "X" to the model designation, i. e., SX-4. In September the revised Super Sky Rider, a nine tube set designated the SX-9, was the first communications receiver to use metal tubes and iron core IF transformers. From 1936 Hallicrafters offered a complete line of receivers starting with the $29.50 Sky Buddy. By the end of the decade the model numbers had reached SX-24. The Super Skyrider line went on to include the SX-11, SX-16, SX-17, SX-28 and SX-28A.

During this period Hallicrafters specialized in giving the most possible features for the dollar and in bringing new developments to the market in the fastest possible time. They did this by using almost all purchased components, capitalizing wherever possible on the low-priced, high-volume parts devel-

HALLICRAFTERS

HALLICRAFTERS

oped for broadcast receivers.

World War II came and Hallicrafters changed over to war production. Many of the prewar Hallicrafters receivers and transmitters were used almost as is for wartime communications. The company produced 50,000 SX-28s and 18,000 HT-4 transmitters for the war effort. The S-29 portable receiver and the S-36 VHF receiver were also produced in volume.

After the war Hallicrafters plunged back into the amateur communications business with a long line of new models. At the low end of the line was the S-38, the successor to the Sky Buddy, which appeared to be a repackaged Echophone EC-1A. The first top-of-the-line postwar model was the SX-42, the first receiver to use the new miniature tubes developed during the war. It used two 6AG5's as RF amplifiers.

In the late 1940's the company returned to the consumer field for the first time since 1934 with a line of television receivers and high fidelity receivers and amplifiers. The market turned out to be too competitive and unprofitable and the line was soon dropped.

The 1950's were troubled but innovative years for Hallicrafters. Bill Halligan sold the company and then bought it back again. The S-76, introduced in 1951, was the first of a long line of double conversion receivers using the dual intermediate frequencies of 1650 and 50 kHz. The 50 kHc L/C circuits provided for a versatile, switchable selectivity system. By the end of the decade the receiver model numbers had reached SX-111 and the line of great receivers was almost at its end.

Northrop Corporation acquired Hallicrafters in the mid-1960's and located it in Rolling Meadows, Ill., where it became largely a defense electronics manufacturer. It was moved to Dallas in 1966. Hallicrafters had peak sales of $200 million in the late 1960's but then declined sharply.

In 1972 sales dropped to 50% of the 1970 level.

Northrop got rid of Hallicrafters and the company went through a series of owners in the 1970's. Sales had dropped to $1.3 million in 1979 when the company stopped doing business. The last mention of Hallicrafters came in an item in Electronic News in June, 1980. which said that Hallicrafters would resume business in a new plant in Miami. Nothing further has been heard of the company.

William J. Halligan, W9AC, is long retired and divides his time between Miami and Chicago.

MODEL: H-13 YRS: 1933 REMARKS: Believed same as Z-13.

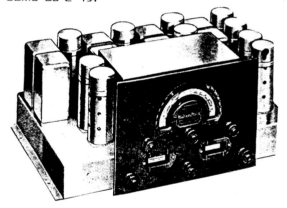

MODEL: Z-13 All-Wave Superhet YRS: 1933 BANDS: 4 IF: 465 kHz TUBES: 13 REMARKS: Manufactured by Silver-Marshall. BC type receiver with separate audio amplifier and power supply. Used "Clough Quadro-tuned IF System."

HALLICRAFTERS

MODEL: Z-10 YRS: 1934 PRICE: $86.50 for chassis and speaker BANDS: 4, .525-30 mHz IF: 465 kHz FILTER: None TUBES: 7, 2A7 conv, 58 if, 2B7 if/det/avc, 58 bfo, 2 2A5 af out, 5Z3 rect AF OUT: 5 W. REMARKS: Mfg by Silver-Marshall, BC type receiver.

MODEL: Z-DELUXE All Wave Super YRS: 1934 PRICE: $139.50 for chassis and 12" speaker BANDS: .150-23 mHz IF: 465 kHz FILTER: None TUBES: 13, 6 '56, 4 '58, 2 2A5, 1 5Z3 REMARKS: Mfg by Silver-Marshall, BC type receiver.

MODEL: S-1 Sky-Rider YRS: 1934 PRICE: $39.95 BANDS: 4, 1.5-25 mHz TYPE: Regenerative TRF FILTER: None TUBES: 5, 6D6 rf, 6D6 regen det, 6C6 af1, 42 af out, 80 rect

MODEL: S-1 Skyrider "special" YRS: 1934 PRICE: $49.95 REMARKS: Same as S-1 Sky-rider with addition of bandspread control

MODEL: S-1 Skyrider "standard" battery model PRICE: $42.50 REMARKS: Tube line-up not known.

HALLICRAFTERS

MODEL: S-1 Skyrider "special' battery model PRICE: $59.50 REMARKS: Tube lineup not known.

MODEL: Skyrider "standard" (1935 model) YRS: 1934-35 PRICE: $39.95 REMARKS: Same as S-1 Skyrider "special".

MODEL: Super Sky-Rider YRS: 1934-35 PRICE: $59.95 TUBES: 7 AF OUT: 3 W. REMARKS: Part of "the new Hallicrafters 1935 line," internal speaker, differs from the S/SX-4 series in that S-4 has added knob to right of speaker and eliminated the bottom center knob.

MODEL: De Luxe All Wave Superhet YRS: 1934-35 BANDS: .15-23 mHz REMARKS: BC type receiver, part of "the new Hallicrafters 1935 line."

MODEL: S/SX-4 Super Skyrider YRS: 1935 PRICE: $59.95, $68.95 w/xtal BANDS: 4, 1.3-21 mHz IF: 465 kHz FILTER: "S" none, "SX" xtal TUBES: 7, 6D6 rf, 6A7 conv, 2 6D6 if, 6F7 det/bfo, 42 af out, 80 rect AF OUT: 3 W. REMARKS: Internal speaker.

HALLICRAFTERS

MODEL: S/SX-5 Super Skyrider PRICE: $69.95, $79.95 w/xtal BANDS: 5, .54-21 mHz REMARKS: Same as S/SX-4 except price and band coverage.

MODEL: S/SX-6 Super Skyrider PRICE: $69.95, $78.95 w/xtal BANDS: 5, 1.3-30 mHz REMARKS: Same as S/SX-4 except for price and band coverage.

MODEL: S/SX-7 Super Skyrider YRS: 1935 PRICE: $79.50, $89.50 w/xtal BANDS: 5, .54-48 mHz IF: 465 kHz FILTER: "S" none, "SX" xtal TUBES: 9 REMARKS: Internal speaker, only reference in Dachis list, similar to S-9.

MODEL: S-8/S-8A YRS: 1935 PRICE: $49.50 BANDS: 3, .54-17 mHz IF: 465 kHz FILTER: None TUBES: 7 REMARKS: Airplane dial, similar to Super-7 (q.v.), probably built by RCA for Hallicrafters, internal speaker.

MODEL: S/SX-9 Super Skyrider YRS: 1935-36 PRICE: $79.50, $89.50 w/xtal BANDS: 5, .54-41 mHz IF: 465 kHz FILTER: "S" none, "SX" xtal TUBES: 9, 6K7 rf, 6L7 mix, 6C5 hfo, 6K7 if, 6H6 det/avc, 6K7 bfo, 6F5 af1, 6F6 af out, 5Z4 rect REMARKS: Internal speaker, first metal tube and first iron core IF receiver, round external dial.

HALLICRAFTERS

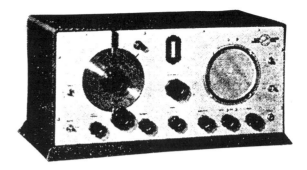

MODEL: S/SX-9 Super Skyrider (Variation) YRS: 1936 REMARKS: Pictured in March and April 1936 QST and in CQ, May 1983, p. 13 (Dachis collection) where it is identified as SX-9. Differs from above SX-9 as has winged Hallicrafters emblem in upper right corner and has very different front panel layout. Compare with pictures of SX-9 in January and June, 1936, QST.

MODEL: Super-7 YRS: 1935 PRICE: $49.50 BANDS: 3, .55-21 mHz IF: 465 kHz FILTER: None TUBES: 7, 78 rf, 6A7 conv, 78 if, 75 det/avc/af1, 78 bfo, 42 af out, 80 rect REMARKS: Internal speaker, airplane dial, probably manufactured by RCA, similar to S-8/A, appears identical to Montgomery-Ward Super-7.

HALLICRAFTERS

MODEL: 5-T Sky-Buddy YRS: 1936 PRICE: $29.50 BANDS: 3, .55-16 mHz IF: 465 kHz FILTER: None TUBES: 5, 6A7 conv, 6F7 if/bfo, 75 det/avc/af1, 42 af out, 80 rect REMARKS: Internal speaker, airplane dial.

MODEL: S/SX-10, Ultra-Skyrider YRS: 1936 PRICE: $99.50, $114.50 w/xtal BANDS: 4, 5.5-79 mHz IF: 1600 kHz FILTER: xtal "X" version only TUBES: 10, 6K7 rf, 6L7 mix, 6C5 hfo, 6K7 if1, 6L7 if2, 6R7 det/avc/bfo, 6J7 noise amp, 6Q7 noise rect/af1, 6F6 af out, 5Z4 rect AF OUT: 3.5 W. REMARKS: Less than 200 made.

MODEL: S/SX-11 Super Skyrider YRS: 1936-37 PRICE: $89.50, $99.50 with crystal BANDS: 5, .535-40 mHz IF: 465 kHz FILTER: Crystal in "X" version TUBES: 11, 6K7 rf, 6L7 mix, 6C5 hfo, 2 6K7 if, 6R7 det/avc/af1, 6K7 bfo, 6G5 tun eye, 2 6L6 p/p af out, 5Z3 rect AF OUT: 14 W. REMARKS: Magic eye tuning indicator, first Super Skyrider with separate speaker.

HALLICRAFTERS

MODEL: S/SX-12 Sky Rider Commercial YRS: 1936 PRICE: $99.50, $114.50 with crystal BANDS: 5, 0.1-11.5 mHz IF: 1600 kHz FILTER: Crystal in "X" version TUBES: 11, 6K7 rf, 6L7 mix, 6C5 hfo, 2 6K7 if, 6R7 det/avc/af1, 6K7 bfo, 6G5 tun eye, 2 6L6 p/p af out, 5Z3 rect AF OUT: 14 W.

MODEL: S-14 Sky Chief YRS: 1936 PRICE: $44.50 BANDS: 3, .54-17.6 mHz IF: 465 kHz FILTER: None TUBES: 7, 78 rf, 6A7 conv, 6F7 if/bfo, 75 det/avc/af1, 42 af out, 6G5 tun eye, 80 rect REMARKS: Internal speaker, tuning eye, airplane dial. Note two different panel layouts.

MODEL: S-14 Sky Chief (Variation) REMARKS: 6D6 rf (vs 78), 6B5 af out (vs 42)

HALLICRAFTERS

MODEL: Sky Master YRS: 1937 BANDS: 3, .53-17 mHz TUBES: 8 REMARKS: Airplane dial, tuner for amateur or BC use with amplifier or headphones.

MODEL: S/SX-15 Sky Challenger YRS: 1937 PRICE: $69.50, $81.95 w/xtal BANDS: 5, .535-38 mHz IF: 465 kHz FILTER: xtal "X" version only TUBES: 9, 6K7 rf, 6L7 mix, 6C5 hfo, 2 6K7 if, 6Q7 det/avc/af1, 6K7 bfo, 6F6G af out, 80 rect AF OUT: 4 W

MODEL: S/SX-16 Super Skyrider YRS: 1937-38 PRICE: $99.00, $111.00 w/xtal BANDS: 6, .55-60 mHz IF: 465 kHz FILTER: xtal, "X" version only TUBES: 11, 6K7 rf, 6L7 mix, 6J5 hfo, 2 6K7 if, 6R7 det/avc/af1, 6J7 bfo, 6J7 meter amp, 2 6V6 p/p af out, 5Z3 rect AF OUT: 13 W.

HALLICRAFTERS

MODEL: S/SX-17 Super Skyrider YRS: 1938-39 PRICE: $125.50, $137.50 w/xtal BANDS: 6, .54-62 mHz IF: 465 kHz FILTER: xtal "X" version only TUBES: 13, 2 6K7 rf, 6L7 mix, 6J5 hfo, 2 6K7 if, 6R7 det/ avc/af1, 6J7 meter amp, 6J7 bfo, 6J5 nl, 2 6V6 p/p af out, 5Z3 rect AF OUT: 13 W. REMARKS: Same as SX-16 except noise limiter switch on front panel plus two rf amplifier stages.

MODEL: SX-17F YRS: 1937 PRICE: $137.50 TUBES: 12 REMARKS: Same as SX-17 except only 12 tubes, probably built special for FCC. Per Dachis list.

MODEL: S/SX-18 Sky Challenger II YRS: 1938 PRICE: $77.00, $89.00 w/xtal BANDS: 5, .54-38 mHz IF: 465 kHz FILTER: xtal "X" version only TUBES: 9, 6K7 rf, 6L7 mix, 6J5 hfo, 2 6K7 if, 6Q7 det/avc/af1, 6J7 bfo, 6F6 af out, 80 rect REMARKS: Infinite image rejection circuit, recessed main dial. AF OUT: 3.5 W.

HALLICRAFTERS

HALLICRAFTERS

MODEL: DD-1 Skyrider Diversity (Proto-type) YRS: 1938 BANDS: 6, 545-62 mHz IF: 465 kHz FILTER: Tunable notch filters (infinite IF Rejection System) TUBES: 25, 4 1851 rf, 2 6L7 mix, 6K6 hfo, 2 6K7 if, 2 6L7 if, 6J5 heterotone osc, 2 6H6 det/avc, 2 6H6 nl, 6J7 "S" meter amp, 2 6J7 div meter amp, 2 6J5 af1/af2, 2 2A3 p/p af out, 2 5Z3 rect REMARKS: Separate power supply and audio chassis. This is the receiver pictured in all Hallicrafter ads for the DD-1. AF OUT: 10 W.

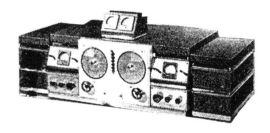

MODEL: DD-1 Skyrider Diversity (Variation #1) YRS: 1938-40 PRICE: $422 TUBES: 26, same as DD-1 (Prototype) except added 6J5 bfo REMARKS: Added BFO, replaced separate A and B RF gain controls with single RF balance control, added a BFO pitch control and changed the positions of several of the controls. This is the model that was actually delivered. Best estimate is only about 100 made.

MODEL: DD-1 Skyrider Diversity (Variation #2) REMARKS: Same as Variation #1 but with streamilined appendages added to the top of the main tuner unit. They contained nothing but the two diversity meters. Note that the photo above is of the prototype unit with the appendages.

MODEL: S-19 Sky Buddy YRS: 1938 PRICE: $29.50 BANDS: 3, .548-18.5 mHz IF: 465 kHz FILTER: None TUBES: 5, 6K8 conv, 6P7 if/bfo, 6Q7 det/avc/af1, 6K6 af out, 80 rect REMARKS: Over 10,000 built, internal speaker, single tuning knob, recessed dial. 6L7 if/bfo used on some models.

MODEL: S-19R Sky Buddy YRS: 1939-42 PRICE: $29.50 BANDS: 4, .545-44 mHz IF: 455 kHz FILTER: None TUBES: 6, 6K8 conv, 6SK7 if, 76 bfo, 6SQ7 det/avc/af1, 42(6F6) af out, 80 rect REMARKS: Internal speaker. Added bandspread knob, 10 meter band, separate BFO tube. "Over 12,000 purchased per QST 9/39.

HALLICRAFTERS

MODEL: S-20 Sky Champion <u>YRS</u>: 1938-39
<u>PRICE</u>: $49.50 <u>BANDS</u>: 4, .545-44 mHz <u>IF</u>: 455
kHz <u>FILTER</u>: None <u>TUBES</u>: 8, 6K7 rf, 6L7
mix, 6J5 hfo, 6K7 if, 6Q7 det/avc/af1, 6J5
bfo, 6F6 af out, 80 rect <u>REMARKS</u>: Internal speaker, single tuning knob, recessed
dial.

MODEL: S-20R Sky Champion <u>YRS</u>: 1939-45
<u>PRICE</u>: $49.50 <u>BANDS</u>: 4, .545-44 mHz <u>IF</u>:
455 kHz <u>FILTER</u>: None <u>TUBES</u>: 9, 6SK7 rf,
6K8 conv, 2 6SK7 if, 6SQ7 det/avc/af1,
6H6 nl, 6J5 bfo, 6F6 af out, 80 rect <u>AF
OUT</u>: 3 W. REMARKS: Internal speaker,
covered dial, two tuning knobs, additional if stage over S-20.

HALLICRAFTERS

MODEL: S-21 Skyrider 5-10 <u>YRS</u>: 1938-39
<u>PRICE</u>: $69.50 <u>BANDS</u>: 2, 27-68 mHz <u>IF</u>: 1600
kHz <u>FILTER</u>: None <u>TUBES</u>: 9, 1852 rf, 6L7
mix, 6J5 hfo, 6K7 if, 6P7 if/bfo, 6Q7 det/
avc/af1, 6H6 nl, 6F6 af out, 80 rect
<u>REMARKS</u>: Internal speaker, single tun-
ing knob.

MODEL: S-22 Skyrider Marine <u>YRS</u>: 1938
<u>PRICE</u>: $64.50 <u>BANDS</u>: 4, .14-18.5 mHz <u>IF</u>:
1600 kHz <u>FILTER</u>: None <u>TUBES</u>: 8, 6K7 rf,
6L7 mix, 6J5 hfo, 6K7 if, 6Q7 det/avc/af1,
6J5 bfo, 25L6 af out, 25Z5 rect <u>REM-
ARKS</u>: AC/DC, internal speaker. Dachis
list shows 455 kHz IF.

MODEL: S-22R Skyrider Marine <u>YRS</u>: 1940-
46 <u>PRICE</u>: $64.50 <u>BANDS</u>: 4, .11-18.5 mHz ,
<u>IF</u>: 1600 kHz <u>FILTER</u>: None <u>TUBES</u>: 8,
6SK7 rf, 6K8 conv, 2 6SK7 if, 6SQ7 det/
avc/af1, 6J5 bfo, 25L6 af out, 25Z5 rect
<u>REMARKS</u>: Internal speaker, AC/DC,
covered dial.

HALLICRAFTERS

MODEL: SX-23 Skyrider 23 YRS: 1939
PRICE: $115.50 BANDS: 4 GC, .54-34 mHz,
4 ham bands 80, 40, 20, 10 mtrs I F: 455
kHz FILTER: xtal TUBES: 11, 6SK7 rf,
6SA7 mix, 6SJ7 hfo, 2 6SK7 if, 6SQ7 det/
af1, 6B8 avc amp/rect, 6SJ7 bfo, 6H6 nl,
6F6 af out, 80 rect AF OUT: 5 W.

MODEL: SX-24 Skyrider Defiant YRS: 1939-
43 PRICE: $69.50 BANDS: 4, .54-43 mHz IF:
455 kHz FILTER: Crystal TUBES: 9, 6SK7 rf,
6K8 conv, 2 6SK7 if, 6SQ7 det/avc/af1, 6H6
anl, 76 bfo, 6F6 af out, 80 rect

MODEL: SX-25 Super Defiant YRS: 1940-46
PRICE: $99.50 BANDS: 4, .54-42 mHz
IF: 455 kHz FILTER: xtal TUBES: 12, 6SK7
rf1, 6SK7 rf2, 6K8 conv, 2 6SK7 if, 6SQ7
det/avc/af1, 6SQ7 phase inv, 6H6 nl,
6J5 bfo, 2 6F6 p/p af out, 80 rect AF
OUT: 8 W.

HALLICRAFTERS

MODEL: S-26F YRS: 1938 BANDS: 2, 27-82
mHz IF: 1600 kHz TUBES: 8 REMARKS:
Electrically like S-21, custom built for
FCC, per Dachis list.

MODEL: S-27 YRS: 1940-43 PRICE: $175.00
BANDS: 3, 27-145 mHz IF: 5250 kHz
FILTER: None TUBES: 15, 956 rf, 954 mix,
955 hfo, 1853 if1, 1852 if2, 6SK7 if3,
6H6 det/avc, 6J5 bfo, 6C8 phase inv,
6D8 af1, 1852 lim, 6H6 disc, 2 6V6 p/p af
out, VR150 vr, 5Z3 rect REMARKS: AM/
FM/CW.

MODEL: S-27B YRS: 1940-41 BANDS: 3,
36-165 mHz REMARKS: Same as S-27 except for frequency coverage.

MODEL: S-27FCC YRS: 1942 REMARKS:
Special S-27 for FCC per Dachis list.

MODEL: SX-28 Super Skyrider YRS: 1940-43
PRICE: $159.50 BANDS: 6, .54-43 mHz IF:
455 kHz FILTER: Crystal TUBES: 15, 6AB7
rf1, 6SK7 rf2, 6SA7 mix, 6SA7 hfo, 6L7 if1/
nl, 6SK7 if2, 6B8 det/meter amp, 6B8 avc
amp, 6AB7 noise amp, 6H6 noise rect, 6J5
bfo, 6SC7 af1, 2 6V6 p/p af out, 5Z3 rect
AF OUT: 8 W. REMARKS: "Over 50,000 built"
- probably includes "A" model.

HALLICRAFTERS

MODEL: SX-28A Super Skyrider YRS: 1944-46 PRICE: $223 REMARKS: Same as SX-28 except added permeability tuned, higher Q inductors in front end. The inductors and trimmers for each band were mounted on small, individual chasses for easy removal.

MODEL: SX-28FCC REMARKS: Special SX-28 manufactured for FCC. Differences not known.

MODEL: S-29 Sky Traveler YRS: 1940-43 PRICE: $59.50 BANDS: 4, .55-30 mHz IF: 455 kHz FILTER: None TUBES: 9, 1T4 rf, 1R5 conv, 2 1P5 if, 1H5 det/af1, 1G4 bfo, 1G4 avc, 3Q4 af out, 50Y6 rect REMARKS: Portable, AC/DC/batteries, internal speaker. 10,000 built mostly during World War II.

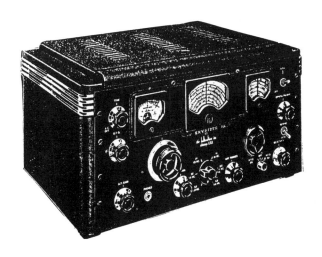

MODEL: S-30 Radio Compass YRS: 1940-43 PRICE: $99.50 BANDS: 3, 0.2-3 mHz IF: 175 kHz FILTER: None TUBES: 6, 6SK7 rf, 6K8 conv, 6SK7 if, 6SQ7 det/avc/af1, 6G6 af out, 6U5 tun eye REMARKS: Direction finding receiver, 6 W. vibrapack power supply.

MODEL: SX-32 Skyrider 32 YRS: 1941-43 PRICE: $149.50 BANDS: 6, .54-40 mHz IF: 455 kHz FILTER: Crystal TUBES: 13, 6AB7/1853 rf1, 6SK7 rf2, 6BA7 mix, 6SA7 hfo, 6K7 if1, 6SK7 if2, 6H6 det/nl, 6J5 bfo, 6B8 avc amp/rect, 6SC7 af1, 2 6V6 af out, 5Z3 rect

HALLICRAFTERS

MODEL: S-33 Sky Trainer Transceiver
YRS: 1943 PRICE: $29.50 BANDS: 1, 112-118
mHz TUBES: 3 REMARKS: Internal speaker,
battery operated.

MODEL: S-35 Panoramic Receiver YRS:
1942-46 PRICE: $375.50 IF: 455, 100 kHz
TUBES: 14, 6SG7 if, 6SA7 conv, 6SK7 if,
6SQ7 det/vert amp, 6SN7 sawtooth osc,
6SJ7 blanking, 6AC7 reac mod, 6J5 osc,
6SC7 hor amp, 2X2/879 hv rect, 80 lv
rect, VR105 vr, VR150 vr, 5AP1 crt REM-
ARKS: 455 kHz input panoramic adaptor.

MODEL: S-36 YRS: 1942 PRICE: $307.50
BANDS: 3, 27.8-143 mHz IF: 5250 kHz FILT-
ER: None TUBES: 15 REMARKS: Similar to
S-27 (q.v.) and ARR-5.

HALLICRAFTERS

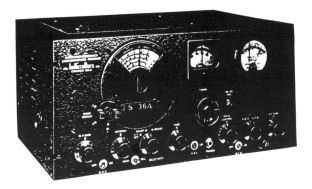

MODEL: S-36A YRS: 1945-46 PRICE: $415
BANDS: 3, 27.8-143 mHz IF: 5250 kHz FILT-
ER: None TUBES: 15, 956 rf, 954 mix, 955
hfo, 6AC7/1852 if1, 6AB7/1853 if2, 6SK7
if3, 6H6 det/nl, 6AC7/1852 FM lim, 6H6 FM
disc, 6SL7 af1, 6J5 bfo, 2 6V6 p/p af out
VR150 vr, 5U4 rect REMARKS: AM/FM/CW,
similar to S-27, BC-787.

MODEL: S-37 YRS: 1945-48 PRICE: $591.75
BANDS: 1, 130-210 mHz IF: 18 mHz FILTER:
None TUBES: 14, 2 954 rf, 954 mix, 955
hfo, 6AC7/1852 if1, 6AB7/1853 if2, 6SK7
if3, 6H6 det/nl, 6AC7/1852 FM lim, 6H6 FM
disc, 6SC7 af1, 6V6 af out, VR150 vr, 5U4
rect REMARKS: AM/FM.

HALLICRAFTERS

MODEL: S-38 YRS: 1946 PRICE: $39.50
BANDS: 4, .54-32 mHz IF: 455 kHz FILTER:
None TUBES: 6, 12SA7 conv, 12SK7 if,
12SQ7 det/avc/af1, 12SQ7 bfo/nl, 35L6
af out, 35Z5 rect AF OUT: 1.6 W. REMARKS:
AC/DC, internal speaker. Appears to be
repackaged Echophone EC-1A. (qv)

MODEL: S-38A YRS: 1946-47 PRICE: $49.50
BANDS: 4, .54-30 mHz IF: 455 kHz FILTER:
None TUBES: 5, 12SA7 conv, 12SA7 if/bfo,
12SQ7 det/avc/af1, 50L6 af out, 35Z5 rect
REMARKS: AC/DC, internal speaker.

MODEL: S-38B YRS: 1947-52 PRICE: $49.50
BANDS: 4, .54-32 mHz IF: 455 kHz FILTER:
None TUBES: 5, 12SA7 conv, 12SK7 if/bfo,
12SQ7 det/avc, 35L6 af out, 35Z5 rect RE-
MARKS: AC/DC, internal speaker.

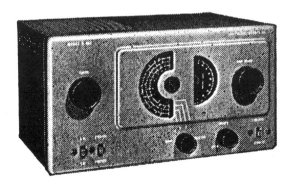

MODEL: S-38C YRS: 1952-54 PRICE: $49.50
BANDS: 4, .54-32 mHz IF: 455 kHz FILTER:
None TUBES: 5, 12SA7 conv, 12SK7 if/bfo,
12SQ7 det/avc, 50L6 af out, 35Z5 rect RE-
MARKS: AC/DC, internal speaker.

HALLICRAFTERS

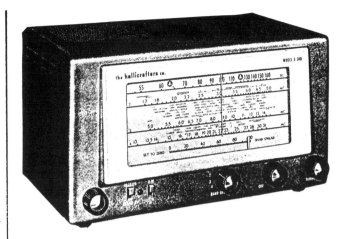

MODEL: S-38D YRS: 1954-57 PRICE: $49.50
BANDS: 4, .54-32 mHz IF: 455 kHz FILTER:
None TUBES: 5, 12SA7 conv, 12SG7 if/bfo,
12SQ7 det/af1, 50L6 af out, 35Z5 rect AF
OUT: 1 W. REMARKS: Changed to slide rule
dial, AC/DC, internal speaker.

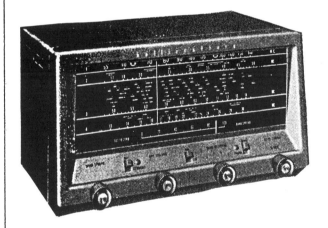

MODEL: S-38E YRS: 1957-61 PRICE: $54.95
BANDS: 4, .54-32 mHz IF: 455 kHz FILTER:
None TUBES: 5, 12BE6 conv, 12BA6 if/bfo,
12AU6 det/af1, 50C5 af out, 35W4 rect AF
OUT: 1 W. REMARKS: Changed to miniature
tubes, AC/DC, internal speaker.

MODEL: S-38EB (sometimes S-38B) REMARKS:
S-38E in blond cabinet.

MODEL: S-38EM (Sometimes S-38M) REMARKS:
S-38E in mahogany cabinet.

MODEL: SX-38 YRS: 1944 PRICE: $225 REM-
ARKS: Similar to SX-28. Only mention in
Dachis list.

HALLICRAFTERS

MODEL: S-39 Sky Ranger YRS: 1945-46
PRICE: $110 BANDS: 4, .54-30.5 mHz IF: 455
kHz FILTER: None TUBES: 9, 1T4 rf, 1R5
conv, 1 1P5 if, 1H5 det/avc/af1, 1H5 bfo/
anl, 3Q5 af out, 2 35Z5 rect REMARKS:
Portable, AC/DC/Battery, similar to S-29.

MODEL: S-40 YRS: 1946-47 PRICE: $79.50
BANDS: 4, .54-43 mHz IF: 455 kHz FILTER:
None TUBES: 9, 6SG7 rf, 6SA7 conv, 2 6SK7
if, 6SQ7 det/af1, 6H6 avc/anl, 6J5 bfo,
6F6 af out, 80 rect AF OUT: 2.5 W. REM-
ARKS: Internal speaker, updated S-20R.

HALLICRAFTERS

MODEL: S-40A YRS: 1947-49 PRICE: $89.50
BANDS: 4, .54-43 mHz IF: 455 kHz FILTER:
None TUBES: 9, 6SG7 rf, 6SA7 conv, 2 6SK7
if, 6SQ7 det/af1/avc, 6H6 anl/gas gate,
6J5 bfo, 6F6 af out, 5Y3 rect AF OUT:
2.5 W. REMARKS: Internal speaker.

MODEL: S-40AU REMARKS: Same as S-40A
except 105-250 V., 25-60 Hz power supply.

MODEL: S-40B YRS: 1950-54 PRICE: $89.95
('50), $129.95 ('53) BANDS: 4, .54-43 mHz
IF: 455 kHz FILTER: None TUBES: 8, 6SG7
rf, 6SA7 conv, 2 6SK7 if, 6SL7 bfo/det,
6H6 anl/avc, 6F6 af out, 5Y3 rect REM-
ARKS: Internal speaker, "World's most
popular ham receiver" per Hallicrafters'
ad in 1950.

MODEL: S-40BU REMARKS: Same as S-40B
except 105/250 V., 25/60 Hz power supply.

MODEL: S-40B (Variation) REMARKS: Same
as S-40B except following tubes: 6H6 det/
anl/avc, 6SC7 bfo/af1, 6K6 af out

HALLICRAFTERS

MODEL: S-41 Skyrider, Jr. YRS: 1946-47
PRICE: $33.50 BANDS: 3, .55-30 mHz IF: 455
kHz FILTER: None TUBES: 6, 12SA7 conv,
12SK7 if, 12SQ7 det/avc/af1, 12SQ7 bfo/
anl, 35L6 af out, 35Z5 rect REMARKS: AC/
DC, internal speaker, "successor to
EC-1."

MODEL: S-41G REMARKS: S-41 in gray cabinet.

MODEL: S-41W REMARKS: S-41 in white
cabinet.

MODEL: SX-42 YRS: 1946-48 PRICE: $250,
$275 ('48) BANDS: 6, .54-110 mHz IF: 10.7
mHz (FM), 455 kHz (AM) FILTER: Crystal
TUBES: 15, 2 6AG5 rf, 7F8 conv, 6SK7 if1,
6SG7 if2, 6H6 det/nl, 2 7H7 FM limiter, 6H6
FM disc, 6SL7 af inv, 7A4 bfo/FM mtr amp,
2 6V6 p/p af out, VR150 vr, 5U4 rect AF
OUT: 8 W. REMARKS: FM 27-110 mHz.

MODEL: SX-42U REMARKS: SX-42 with 120/
240 V. power supply.

HALLICRAFTERS

MODEL: SX-43 YRS: 1947-49 PRICE: $169.50
BANDS: AM 6, .54-55 mHz, FM 2, .44-55, 88-
108 mHz IF: 455 kHz (AM), 10.7 mHz (FM)
FILTER: Crystal TUBES: 11, 6BA6 rf, 7F8
conv, 6SG7 if1, 6SH7 if2/conv2, 6SH7 if3,
6H6 det/nl, 6AL5 FM ratio det, 6SQ7 af1,
6J5 bfo/osc2, 6V6 af out, 5Y3 rect.

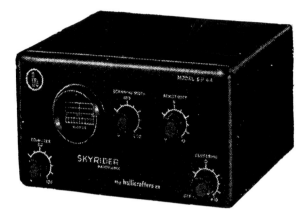

MODEL: SP-44 Skyrider Panoramic YRS:
1947-48 PRICE: $49.50 IF: 450-470 kHz
TUBES: 10 REMARKS: Panoramic adaptor.

MODEL: S-51 Sea-Farer YRS: 1947-49 PRICE:
$129.95 BANDS: 4, .132-13 mHz IF: 455 kHz
FILTER: None TUBES: 10, 6SS7 rf, 7A8
conv, 2 6SS7 if, 7C6 det/avc/af1, 7A6 nl,
6SS7 bfo, 6V6 af out, 35L6 af out, 35Z5
rect REMARKS: AC/DC, internal speaker,
also has 3 fixed frequencies.

HALLICRAFTERS

MODEL: S-52 YRS: 1948-49 PRICE: $99.50
BANDS: 4, 154-43 mHz IF: 455 kHz FILTER:
None TUBES: 8, 6SG7 rf, 6SA7 conv, 2 6SK7
if, 6H6 det/avc, 6SC7 bfo/af1, 25L6 af
out, 25Z6 rect REMARKS: AC/DC version
of S-40A, internal speaker.

MODEL: S-53 YRS: 1948-49 PRICE: $79.50
BANDS: 5, .54-38, 48-54.5 mHz IF: 2075 kHz
FILTER: None TUBES: 8, 6BA6 mix, 6C4 hfo,
2 6BA6 if, 6H6 det/avc/nl, 6SC7 bfo/af1,
6K6 af out, 5Y3 rect AF OUT: 2.5 W. REM-
ARKS: Internal speaker.

MODEL: S-53U REMARKS: Same as S-53 except power supply for 110/130/150/220/
250 V., 25-60 Hz.

MODEL: S-53A YRS: 1950-59 PRICE: $79.95
BANDS: 5, .54-54.5 mHz IF: 455 kHz FILTER:
None TUBES: 8, 6BA6 mix, 6C4 hfo, 2 6BA6
if, 6H6 anl/avc/det, 6SC7 bfo/af1, 6K6
af out, 5Y3 rect AF OUT: 1 W. REMARKS:
Internal speaker.

MODEL: S-53AU REMARKS: Same as S-53A
except power supply for 110/130/150/220/
250 V., 25-60 kHz.

HALLICRAFTERS

MODEL: SX-62 YRS: 1948-51 PRICE: $269.50
BANDS: 6, .54-109 mHz IF: 455 kHz, except
10.7 mHz bands 5 & 6 (27-109 mHz) FILTER:
Crystal TUBES: 16, 2 6AG5 rf, 7F8 conv,
6SK7 if1, 6SG7 if2, 7H7 if3, 7H7 FM lim/
det, 6H6 FM det, 7A4 bfo, 6H6 nl, 6SL7
af1, 6C4 calib, 2 6V6 p/p af out, VR150
vr, 5U4 rect AF OUT: 10 W. REMARKS: FM
27-109 mHz.

MODEL: SX-62A YRS: 1955-63 PRICE: $350
BANDS: 6, .55-109 mHz IF: 455 kHz bands
1-4, 10.7 mHz bands 5 & 6 (27-109 mHz)
FILTER: Crystal TUBES: 16, 2 6AG5 rf, 7F8
conv, 6SK7 if1, 6SG7 if2, 6SG7 lim/det, 6H6
FM det, 6J5 bfo, 6H6 nl, 2 6SL7 phase inv,
2 6V6 p/p af out, 6C4 calib, VR150 vr, 5U4
rect AF OUT: 10 W. REMARKS: AM/FM
bands 5,6 (27-109 mHz)

MODEL: SX-62B YRS: 1965 PRICE: $525

MODEL: SX-62U PRICE: $279.50 REMARKS:
Same as SX-62 except power supply for
105-250 V., 25-100 Hz.

MODEL: SX-71 YRS: 1949-55 PRICE: $179.50
('49), $249.95 ('55) BANDS: 5, .538-35, 46-56
mHz TYPE: Double conversion, tunable
hfo IF: 2075, 455 kHz FILTER: Crystal
TUBES: 13, 6BA6 rf, 6AU6 mix1, 6C4 hfo,
6BE6 mix2/xco, 3 6SK7 if, 6AL5 det, 6H6
avc/anl, 6SC7 af1/bfo, 6K6 af out, VR150
vr, 5Y3 rect

MODEL: SX-71U REMARKS: Same as SX-71
except power supply for 105-250 V., 25-
100 Hz.

HALLICRAFTERS

HALLICRAFTERS

MODEL: S-72 YRS: 1949-51 PRICE: $79.95
BANDS: 4, .54-31 mHz IF: 455 kHz FILTER:
None TUBES: 8 + rect, 1T4 rf, 1U4 mix, 1R5
hfo, 2 1U4 if, 1U5 det/af1, 1U5 bfo, 3V4
af out, sel rect REMARKS: AC/DC/battery
portable, internal speaker.

MODEL: S-72L YRS: 1950-52 PRICE: $99.95
BANDS: 4, .175-.4, .54-13 mHz IF: 455 kHz
FILTER: None TUBES: 8 + rect, 1T4 rf, 1U4
mix, 1R5 hfo, 2 1U4 if, 1U5 det/af1, 1U5
bfo, 3V4 af out, sel rect REMARKS: Long
wave version of S-72.

MODEL: SX-73 Prototype YRS: 1951 RE-
MARKS: High styled front panel vs mil-
tary style of production receiver. Pictured in 1951 Handbook.

MODEL: SX-73 YRS: 1952-53 PRICE: $975
BANDS: 6, .54-54 mHz TYPE: Double conversion, tunable hfo 7-54 mHz, single
conversion .54-7 mHz IF: 6000, 455 kHz
FILTER: Crystal TUBES: 20, 6AG5 rf1,
6BA6 rf2, 6BE6 mix1, 6C4 hfo, 6BE6 mix2,
6BA6 xco, 4 6BA6 if, 6AL5 det, 6AT6
af1, 6AL5 avc/anl, 6BA6 bfo, 6Y6 af out,
6AG5 xtal cal, 6BA6 if out, VR150 vr,
5U4 rect REMARKS: Military R274/FRR,
similar to SP600. Turret coil selector.

MODEL: S-76 YRS: 1951-54 PRICE: $169.50
('51), $199.95 ('53) BANDS: 4, .538-32 mHz
TYPE: Double conversion, tunable HFO IF:
1650, 50 kHz FILTER: 50 kHz L/C TUBES:
11, 6CB6 rf, 6AU6 mix, 6C4 hfo, 6BA6 if1,
6BE6 conv, 6BA6 if2, 6AL5 det/anl, 6SC7
bfo, 6K6 af out, VR150 vr, 5Y3 rect AF
OUT: 3 W. REMARKS: First of a line of
double conversion receivers using the 50
kHz L/C filter system.

MODEL: S-76U REMARKS: S-76 with universal 105-250 V., 25-60 Hz power supply.

HALLICRAFTERS

MODEL: S-77 YRS: 1950-51 PRICE: $99.50
BANDS: 4, .54-43 mHz IF: 455 kHz FILTER:
None TUBES: 8 REMARKS: AC/DC version
of S-40B, internal speaker.

MODEL: S-77A YRS: 1953 PRICE: $119.95
REMARKS: S-77 with minor electrical
changes.

MODEL: S-85 YRS: 1954-59 PRICE: $119.95
BANDS: 4, .54-34 mHz IF: 455 kHz FILTER:
None TUBES: 8, 6SG7 rf, 6SA7 conv, 2 6SK7
if, 6SC7 bfo/af1, 6H6 nl/avc/det, 6K6 af
out, 5Y3 rect AF OUT: 2 W. REMARKS:
Successor to S-40B - note same tubes.

MODEL: S-85U REMARKS: S-85 with universal 105-250 V., 25-60 Hz power supply.

MODEL: S-86 YRS: 1954-57 PRICE: $119.95
BANDS: 4, .54-34 mHz IF: 455 kHz FILTER:
None TUBES: 8 + ballast, 6SG7 rf, 6SA7
conv, 2 6SK7 if, 6H6 nl/avc/det, 6SC7
bfo/af1, 25L6 af out, 5Y3 rect, ballast
AF OUT: 2 W. REMARKS: AC/DC version of
S-85.

HALLICRAFTERS

MODEL: SX-88 YRS: 1954 PRICE: $595 BANDS:
6, .535-33 mHz TYPE: Double conversion,
tunable HFO IF: 2075, 50 kHz except band
2, 1550, 50 kHz FILTER: 50 kHz L/C TUBES:
20, 6CB6 rf1, 6BA6 rf2, 6U8 mix1/hfo, 6BA6
mix2, 12AX7 xco, 3 6BA6 if, 6AL5 det/nl,
12AX7 af1/phase inv, 6C4 bfo, 6BA6 bfo
buff, 6CB6 avc amp, 12AU7 avc rect/k fol,
2 6V6 p/p af out, 6BA6 calib, 4H4 cur reg,
0D3 vr, 5U4 rect AF OUT: 10 W.

MODEL: SX-88U REMARKS: SX-88 with universal 100-250 V. 25-60 Hz power supply.

MODEL: S-93 YRS: 1954-55 PRICE: $99.95
BANDS: 4, .17-.4, .54-18 mHz IF: 455 kHz
FILTER: None TUBES: 6 + sel rect REMARKS:
AC/DC/Battery portable.

MODEL: SX-96 YRS: 1954-56 PRICE: $249.95
BANDS: 4, .538-34 mHz TYPE: Double conversion, tunable HFO IF: 1650, 50 kHz
FILTER: 50 kHz L/C TUBES: 12, 6CB6 rf,
6AU6 mix, 6C4 hfo, 6BA6 if1, 6BA6 mix2,
12AT7 xco, 6BA6 if2, 6BJ7 det/avc/anl,
6SC7 bfo/af1, 6K6 af out, VR150 vr, 5Y3
rect AF OUT: 1.5 W.

HALLICRAFTERS

HALLICRAFTERS

MODEL: SX-99 YRS: 1954-58 PRICE: $199.95
BANDS: 4, .54-34 mHz IF: 455 kHz FILTER:
Crystal TUBES: 8, 6SG7 rf, 6SA7 conv,
6SG7 if1, 6SK7 if2, 6H6 det/nl/avc, 6SC7
af1/bfo, 6K6 af out, 5Y3 rect AF OUT:
2 W.

MODEL: SX-99U REMARKS: SX-99 with universal 100-250 V., 25-60 Hz power supply.

MODEL: SX-100 YRS: 1955-61 PRICE: $295
BANDS: 4, .54-34 mHz TYPE: Double conversion, tunable HFO IF: 1650, 50 kHz FIL-
TER: 50 kHz L/C TUBES: 14, 6CB6 rf, 6AU6
mix1, 6C4 hfo, 6BA6 mix2, 6BA6 if1, 12AT7
xco, 6C4 if2, 6BA6 if3, 6BJ7 det/avc/nl,
6SC7 af1/bfo, 6K6 af out, 6AU6 calib, 0A2
vr, 5Y3 rect AF OUT: 1.5 W.

MODEL: SX-100 MK1A IF: 1650, 50.5 kHz
REMARKS: Other differences not known.

MODEL: SX-100 MK2 IF: 1650, 50.75 kHz
REMARKS: Other differences not known.

MODEL: SX-101 YRS: 1956-58 PRICE: $395
BANDS: 7 ham bands, 160-10 mtrs TYPE:
Double conversion, tunable HFO IF: 1650,
50 kHz FILTER: 50.5 kHz L/C TUBES: 15, 6CB6
rf, 6BY6 mix1, 12AU7 hfo/buff, 6BA6 if1,
6BA6 mix2, 12AT7 xco, 6C4 if2, 6BA6 if3,
6BJ7 det/nl/avc, 6SC7 af1/bfo, 6BA6 mtr
amp, 6K6 af out, 6AU6 calib, 0A2 vr, 5Y3
rect REMARKS: Ad says, ". . . built like a
battleship. Bigger. Heavier."

MODEL: SX-101 MK II REMARKS: Improved
stability over SX-101. Other differences
not known.

MODEL: SX-101 MK III YRS: 1958 REMARKS:
Oscillator filament always on.

MODEL: SX-101 MK IIIA YRS: 1959 PRICE:
$399.50 BANDS: 7, 80-10 mtrs + 30.5-34.5
converter band TYPE: Double conversion,
tuneable hfo IF: 1650, 50 kHz FILTER: 50.5
kHz L/C TUBES: 15, 6CB6 rf, 6BY6 mix1,
12BY7 hfo, 6BA6 if1, 6BA6 mix2, 12AT7 xco,
6C4 if2, 6BA6 if3, 6BJ7 det/anl/avc, 6SC7
bfo/af1, 6K6 af out, 6AU6 calib, 6BA6 mtr
amp, 0A2 vr, 5Y3 rect REMARKS: 160 meter
band replaced with converter band.

MODEL: SX-101A YRS: 1959-62 PRICE: $399.50
BANDS: 7, 80-10 mtrs + 30.5-34.5 mHz converter band TYPE: Double conversion, tunable hfo IF: 1650, 50.75 kHz FILTER: 50.75
kHz L/C TUBES: 15, 6DC6 rf, 6BY6 mix1,
12BY7A hfo, 6BA6 if1, 6BA6 mix2, 12AT7
xco, 6DC6 1f2, 6BJ7 det/anl/avc, 6BY6 prod
det, 6SC7 af1/bfo, 6K6 af out, 6BA6 mtr
amp, 6AU6 calib, 0A2 vr, 5Y3 rect REM-
ARKS: Changes from SX-101 - new prod
detector, 2 position avc, full 10 meter
bandspread, band to band gain equaliza-
tion.

HALLICRAFTERS

MODEL: S-107 YRS: 1959-61 PRICE: $94.95
BANDS: 5, .54-34, 48-54.5 mHz IF: 455 kHz
FILTER: None TUBES: 8, 6BA6 mix, 6C4 hfo,
2 6BA6 if, 6H6 det/avc/anl, 6SC7 bfo/af1,
6K6 af out, 5Y3 rect AF OUT: 1 W. RE-
MARKS: Built in speaker. Some models
have 6AQ5 audio output tube.

MODEL: S-108 YRS: 159-62 PRICE: $129.95
BANDS: 4, .54-34 mHz IF: 455 kHz FILTER:
None TUBES: 8, 6SG7 rf, 6SA7 conv, 6SG7
if1, 6SK7 if2, 6H6 det/anl/avc, 6SC7 bfo/
af1, 6K6 af out, 5Y3 rect AF OUT: 2 W.
REMARKS: Stripped version of SX-110. Has
no "S" meter, antenna trimmer or crystal
filter and does have internal speaker.

HALLICRAFTERS

MODEL: SX-110 YRS: 1959-62 PRICE: $159.95
BANDS: 4, .54-34 mHz IF: 455 kHz FILTER:
Crystal TUBES: 8, 6SG7 rf, 6SA7 conv, 6SK7
if2, 6SG7 if1, 6H6 det/anl/avc, 6SC7 bfo/
af1, 6K6 af out, 5Y3 rect AF OUT: 2 W.

MODEL: SX-111 (Early version) YRS: 1960-
61 PRICE: $249.50 BANDS: 6, WWV + 80-10
mtrs TYPE: Double conversion, tunable hfo
IF: 1650, 50.75 kHz FILTER: 50.75 kHz L/C
TUBES: 12, 6DC6 rf, 6BY6 mix1, 6C4 hfo,
6CB6 if1, 6BA6 mix2, 12AT7 xco, 6DC6 if2,
6BJ7 det/avc/nl, 12AX7 af1/bfo, 6AQ5 af
out, 0A2 vr, 5Y3 rect

MODEL: SX-111 (Later version) TUBES: 13,
including 6AU6 calib REMARKS: Adds crystal calibrator to original SX-111.

MODEL: SX-111 MK I YRS: 1961-62 PRICE:
$279.50 TYPE: Double conversion, tunable
hfo IF: 1650, 50.75 kHz FILTER: 50.75 kHz
L/C TUBES: 14, 6DC6 rf, 6BY6 mix1, 6C4
hfo, 6CB6 if1, 6BA6 mix2, 12AT7 xco, 6DC6
if2, 6BJ7 det/avc/nl, 6BY6 prod det, 12AX7
af1/bfo, 6AQ5 af out, 6AU6 calib, 0A2 vr,
5Y3 rect REMARKS: Adds product detector to SX-111.

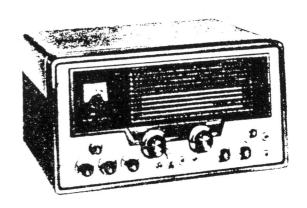

HALLICRAFTERS

MODEL: SX-112 YRS: 1961 PRICE: $595
BANDS: 6, .54-34 mHz TYPE: Double conversion, tunable HFO IF: 1650, 50 kHz FILTER:
50 kHz L/C TUBES: 14

MODEL: SX-115 YRS: 1961-64 PRICE: $595
BANDS: 9 500 kHz bands, WWV + 80-10
mtrs TYPE: Tunable IF, triple conversion
IF: 6005-6505, 1005, 50.75 kHz FILTER:
50.75 kHz L/C TUBES: 18 + 5 Si diodes,
6DC6 rf, 6BA7 mix1, 12AT7 xco, 6DC6 var
if, 6BA7 mix2, 6CB6 vfo, 6DC6 if, 6BA6
mix3, 6DC6 if, 12AX7 af1/var bfo, 6BJ7
anl/det/agc2, 6AQ5 af out, 6AU6 agc amp,
HD6225 agc1, 2 HD6225 cw/ssb anl, 6AU6
calib, 6AU6 mtr amp, 12AT7 xtal bfo,
6BY6 prod det, 2 Si rect, 0A2 vr AF OUT:
1.5 W.

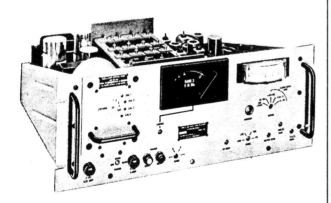

MODEL: SX-116 YRS: 1961 BANDS: 4, 2-30
mHz IF: 1650 kHz FILTER: Crystal lattice
REMARKS: Military quality crystal controlled SSB strip receiver capable of ISB
reception.

HALLICRAFTERS

MODEL: SX-117 YRS: 1962-66 PRICE: $379.95
BANDS: 9 500 kHz bands, 3-30 mHz TYPE:
Tunable IF, triple conversion IF: 6000-
6500, 1650, 50.75 kHz FILTER: 50.75 kHz L/C
TUBES: 13 + 4 Si diodes, 6DC6 rf, 6EA8
mix1/k fol, 12AT7 xco, 6BA6 if1, 6BE6
mix2, 6EA8 vfo/k fol, 6DC6 if2, 6EA8
mix3/SB xco sw osc, 6BA6 if3, 6BE6 prod
det/bfo, 6BN8 det/avc amp/avc rect,
6GW8 af1/af out, 6AU6 calib, 2 HD6225 anl,
2 Si rect REMARKS: 4 additonal 500 kHz
bands available .085-30 mHz with optional
crystals plus two optional crystal controlled positions. Coverage from .085-3
mHz provided with optional HA-10 tuner
shown atop receiver.

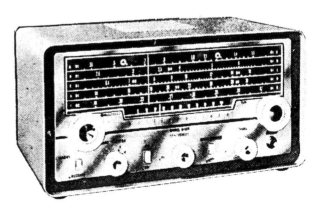

MODEL: S-118 YRS: 1962-65 PRICE: $99.95
BANDS: 5, .185-31 mHz IF: 455 kHz FILTER:
None TUBES: 5 + 2 Si rect REMARKS: In-
ternal speaker.

HALLICRAFTERS

MODEL: S-119 Sky Buddy II YRS: 1961-62
PRICE: $49.95 BANDS: 3, .54-16.4 mHz IF:
455 kHz FILTER: None TUBES: 3 + Si diode
+ Si rect REMARKS: Internal speaker.

MODEL: S-119K Sky Buddy II REMARKS:
Kit version of S-119.

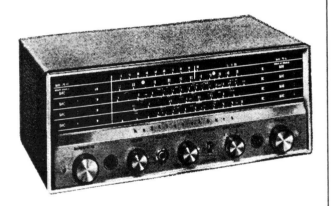

MODEL: S-120 YRS: 1961-65 PRICE: $69.95
BANDS: 4, .54-31 mHz IF: 455 kHz FILTER:
None TUBES: 4 + Si rect, 12BE6 conv,
6BA6 if/bfo, 12AV6 det/avc/af1, 50C5 af
out, si rect REMARKS: AC/DC, internal
speaker, successor to S-38 series.

HALLICRAFTERS

MODEL: SX-122 YRS: 1964-66 PRICE: $295
BANDS: 4, .538-34 mHz TYPE: Double conversion, tunable hfo IF: 1650, 50 kHz FILT-
ER: 50 kHz L/C TUBES: 11 + si diode, 6DC6
r, 6AU6 mix1, 6C4 hfo, 6DC6 if1, 6BL8 mix2/
xco, 6BA6 if2, 6BE6 prod det/bfo, 6BN8
det/agc amp/agc rect, 1N456 anl, 6GW8
af1/af out, 5Y3 rect, 0A2 vr AF OUT: 1 W.

MODEL: SX-122A YRS: 1970 PRICE: $395 REM-
ARKS: Described as advanced SX-122 but
has same tube lineup and external appearance. Perhaps $100 price increase is an
advancement.

MODEL: S-129 YRS: 1965 PRICE: $164.95
BANDS: 4, .54-34 mHz IF: 1650 kHz FILTER:
None TUBES: 7 + 1 diode, 6DC6 rf, 6EA8
mix/hfo, 6EA8 if1, 6BA6 if2, 6BE6 prod det/
bfo, 6AL5 am det/nl, 6GW8 af out, si rect
AF OUT: 2 W. REMARKS: Same as SX-130
less "S" meter and crystal filter.

MODEL: SX-130 YRS: 1965-68 PRICE: $179.95
REMARKS: Same as S-129 with addition of
"S" meter and crystal filter.

HALLICRAFTERS

MODEL: SX-133 YRS: 1967-73 PRICE: $275
BANDS: 4, .535-31.5 mHz FILTER: Crystal
TUBES: 7 REMARKS: Bandspread calibrated
for 80-10 meters plus 49, 31, 25, 19 meter
SW BC bands.

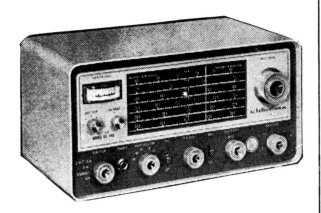

MODEL: SX-140 YRS: 1960-63 PRICE $109.95
BANDS: 6, 80-6 mtr ham bands IF: 1650 kHz
FILTER: None TUBES: 5 + 2 si rect, 6AZ8 rf/
calib, 6U8 mix/hfo, 6BA6 if/bfo, 6T8A det/
avc/anl/af1, 6AW8A af out/mtr amp, 2 si
rect

MODEL: SX-140K REMARKS: SX-140 in kit
form.

MODEL: SX-146 YRS: 1966-68 PRICE: $269.95
BANDS: 10 500 kHz bands, 2-30 mHz TYPE:
Single conversion, pre-mixer IF: 9000 kHz
FILTER: Crystal lattice TUBES: 9 + 3 si
diodes, 6JD6 rf, 12AT7 mix/k fol, 2 6AU6A
if, 12AT7 det/avc/prod det, 12AT7 USB/
LSB bfo, 6GW8 af1/afout, 6BA6 vfo, 6EA8
xco/pre mix, 1N456 anl, 1N456 avc gate,
1N3195 rect

HALLICRAFTERS

MODEL: S-200 Legionaire YRS: 1965-66
PRICE: $59.95 BANDS: 5, BCB + 19, 25, 31,
49 mtrs TUBES: 4 + sel rect, 12BE6 conv,
12BA6 if, 12AV6 det/avc/af1, 50C5 af out,
sel rect REMARKS: Internal speaker.

MODEL: S-210 YRS: 1969 BANDS: 6, BC, 19,
25, 31, 49 mtrs + FM TUBES: 6 REMARKS:
S-200 with FM band added.

MODEL: TW-1000 YRS: 1953 PRICE: $149.95
BANDS: 8, .535-18.3 mHz FILTER: None TUBES:
5 + rect REMARKS: AC/DC/Battery, internal speaker.

MODEL: AN/GRR-2 REMARKS: Signal Corps
SX-28.

MODEL: BC-787B BANDS: 27-140 mHz REM-
ARKS: Military S-36.

MODEL: R-44/ARR-5 BANDS: 3, 27-140 mHz
REMARKS: Airborne version of S-36A, separate power supply.

MODEL: R-45/ARR-7 BANDS: 6, .55-42 mHz
TUBES: 12, 6AB7(1853) rf1, 2 6SK7 rf2 & rf3,
6SA7 mix, 6SA7 hfo, 2 6SK7 if, 6H6 det/avc,

HALLICRAFTERS

6SQ7 af1, 6J5 bfo, 6V6 af out, 0D3/VR-150 vr REMARKS: Airborne version of SX-28A. Many were built by Belmont Radio Co.

MODEL: R-62PR REMARKS: Signal Corps R-29.

MODEL: R-80 REMARKS: Military version of S-29 AC/DC/Battery portable.

MODEL: R-137/GR REMARKS: Signal Corps S-36.

MODEL: R-205/U REMARKS: Signal Corps SX-24.

MODEL: R-210/U REMARKS: Signal Corps S-22R.

MODEL: R-274/FRR REMARKS: Military designation for the SX-73 (and SP-600).

MODEL: RE-1 Sky Courier YRS: 1945 BANDS: 3, .55-19 mHz FILTER: None TUBES: 7, 1R5 conv, 2 1N5 if, 1H5 det/avc/af1, 50L6 af out(AC/DC), 3Q5 af out(battery), 35Z5 rect REMARKS: Portable BC receiver, AC/DC/battery, internal speaker.

HAMMARLUND

Oscar Hammarlund started the Hammarlund Manufacturing Company in 1910. In the 1920's the company, through an affiliate, Hammarlund-Roberts, Inc., manufactured broadcast receivers, and Hammarlund Mfg. Co. marketed components such as variable capacitors, coils and dials. The Hammarlund-Roberts name disappeared about 1932. The two companies used the same address on West 33rd Street in New York City.

Late in 1931 Hammarlund introduced the "Comet" receiver, perhaps the first superheterodyne communications receiver. They followed in the spring of 1932 with the improved "Comet Pro" model which continued in production, with variations, until 1935..

Design of the best known and long lived receiver in the Hammarlund line began in 1933. This was to be the ultimate receiver and was originally called the "Comet Super Pro" but it eventually became simply the Super Pro. Like National, Hammarlund took an uncompromising approach to receiver design. They used special, custom built components. They designed a unique bandswitching system, special IF transformers, and a twelve gang tuning capacitor. Originally scheduled for release in early 1935, the receiver was not ready for delivery until mid-1936.

Hammarlund continuously updated the Super Pro and its descendents were in production until 1973. The original 1936 model was designated the SP-10 series. The SP-100 appeared in 1937, SP-200 in 1939, the SP-400 in 1946 and the SP-600 in 1950. The SP-600 was electrically and physically similar to the SP-10, with the addition of double conversion and rotary turret bandswitching. It was the ultimate refinement of the classic superheterodyne with the tunable HFO.

While Hallicrafters and, to a lesser extent, National, featured a large sel-

HAMMARLUND

ection of receivers spaced $10 or $20 apart across the price spectrum from $29.50 and up, Hammarlund adopted a very conservative approach. The Super Pro, a top-of-the-line receiver, was their only model until 1938 when they brought out the HQ-120 to compete in the medium price range. This, too, became the forerunner of a line of receivers which lasted until 1973. Direct descendents of the HQ-120 were the HQ-129X (1945), HQ-140 (1953), HQ-150 (1956), HQ-160 (1958) and the HQ-180 (1959-73).

Beginning in 1955 Hammarlund manufactured a full line of receivers, most of them bearing the HQ prefix. Only the above models are descendents of the HQ-120. They can be distinguished from less expensive HQ's by their six tuning ranges and elaborate, multi-section variable tuning capacitors.

The only other notable receiver in the Hammarlund line was the PRO-310 which appeared briefly from 1955-57. It was a top-of-the-line receiver with a unique two dial tuning system. For unknown reasons its life was very short.

Time started running out for Hammarlund, as it did for the other communications receiver manufacturers, in the 1950's and 1960's. The company introduced a solid-state ham receiver, the HQ-215, in 1967 but it was not successful and they dropped out of the ham market after that although continuing to sell the HQ-180 SP-600 until about 1973. The Hammarlund name then disappeared from the scene after more than 60 years.

Hammarlund had begun transfering its manufacturing operations from New York City to Mars Hill, NC, in 1951 and completed the move in 1959. By 1965 all the management functions has also moved to Mars Hill. During its final two decades Hammarlund was sold a number of times. Telechrome purchased them in the late 1950's and then sold to Giannini Scientific in 1962 and who in turn sold to Electronic Assistance Corporation in the late 1960's.

HAMMARLUND

Founder Oscar Hammarlund died in 1945. His son, Lloyd A Hammarlund, who had been actively managing the company since the early 1930's, continued the family's involvement. Stuart Meyer, W2GHK, a mobile two-way radio expert, guided the company from 1960 to 1966.

MODEL: Comet YRS: 1931-32 PRICE: $130 chassis, $175 console BANDS: 5, .55-21 mHz IF: 465 kHz TUBES: 8, 224A mix, 227 hfo, 2 235 if, 224A det, 227 bfo, 247 af out, 80 rect REMARKS: Plug-in coils.

MODEL: Comet "All-Wave" YRS: 1932-33 BANDS: 5, .55-21 mHz IF: 465 kHz FILTER: None TUBES: 8, 57 mix, 58 hfo, 2 58 if, 58 bfo, 57 det, 247 af out, 80 rect REMARKS: Plug-in coils, console or table model.

MODEL: Comet Pro (Prototype) YRS: 1932 BANDS: 4, 1.5-21 mHz IF: 465 kHz FILTER: None TUBES: 8 REMARKS: Plug-in coils. Bandsetting caps had external dial scales Inductive coupling between mixer and HFO (coils not shielded). Walnut cabinet.

MODEL: Comet Pro (Variation 1) YRS: 1932
BANDS: 4, 1.5-21 mHz IF: 465 kHz FILTER:
None TUBES: 8, 224A mix, 227 hfo, 2 235
if, 224A det, 227 bfo, 227 af out, 80 rect
REMARKS: Same as prototype except dials
for bandsetting caps are behind panel,
viewed through windows. See QST July,
1932. An optional unit was available containing p/p 245 af out, a speaker and
power supply. Wood cabinet.

MODEL: Comet Pro (Variation 2) YRS: 1932-
33 BANDS: 4, 1.2-20 mHz IF: 465 kHz FILTER:
None TUBES: 8, 57 mix, 58 hfo, 2 58 if, 57
det, 58 bfo, 247 af out, 80 rect REMARKS:
Changes from Variation 1: new tube lineup, electron coupled HFO, metal or wood
cabinet, more selective, full speaker volume, shield cans over plug-in coils.

MODEL: Comet Pro (Variation 2A) YRS:
1932-33 REMARKS: Battery model.

MODEL: Comet Pro (Variation 3) YRS: 1933-
35 PRICE: $88.20 BANDS: 4, 1.5-20 mHz IF:
465 kHz FILTER: None TUBES: 8, 57 mix, 58
hfo, 2 58 if, 57 det, 58 bfo, 2A5 af out 80
rect REMARKS: Changes from Variation 2:
AF output tube changed to 2A5, air tuned
IF transformers, added BFO knob on
panel.

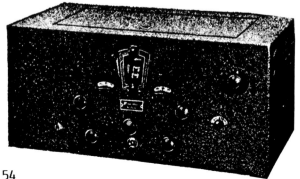

MODEL: Comet Pro (Variation 4) FILTER:
Crystal REMARKS: Same as Variation 3
except adds crystal filter with a crystal
switch and phasing control on panel.

MODEL: Comet Pro (Variation 5) FILTER:
Crystal (Optional) TUBES: 9, 57 mix, 58
hfo, 2 58 if, 57 det, 58 bfo, ? avc, 2A5
af out, 80 rect REMARKS: Differs from
Variations 3 and/or 4 in addition of AVC
tube and switch.

MODEL: Comet Pro (Variation 6) REMARKS:
110 VDC version of Variations 3-5.

MODEL: Comet Pro (Variation 7) REMARKS:
220 VDC version of Variations 3-5.

MODEL: Comet Pro (Variation 8) REMARKS:
Battery powered version of Variations
3-5.

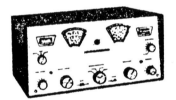

MODEL: HQ-66 YRS: 1964 PRICE: $159.95
BANDS: 4, .54-30 mHz TUBES: 10

MODEL: HQ-88 YRS: 1964 PRICE: $299
BANDS: Ham Bands 160-10 mtrs + WWV
TYPE: Double conversion, tunable hfo IF:
?, 262 kHz FILTER: Q multiplier.

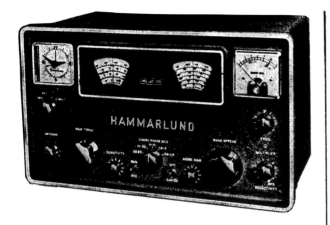

MODEL: HQ-100 YRS: 1956-60 PRICE: $169
BANDS: 4, .54-30 mHz IF: 455 kHz FILTER:
Q Multiplier TUBES: 10, 6BZ6 rf, 6BE6 mix,
6C4 hfo, 2 6BA6 if, 6AL5 det/anl, 12AX7
af1/Q mult/bfo, 6AQ5 af out, OB2 vr,
5Y3 rect

MODEL: HQ-110 YRS: 1957-61 PRICE: $229
BANDS: 7 Ham Bands, 160-6 mtrs TYPE:
Double conversion, tunable hfo IF: 3045,
455 kHz FILTER: Q multiplier TUBES: 12
AF OUT: 1 W.

MODEL: HQ-110C REMARKS: HQ-110 with
clock.

MODEL: HQ-110A YRS: 1962-64 PRICE: $249
BANDS: 7 ham bands, 160-6 mtrs TYPE:
Double conversion, tunable hfo IF: 3045,
455 kHz FILTER: Q multiplier TUBES: 12,
6BZ6 rf, 6BE6 mix1, 6C4 hfo, 6BE6 mix2/
xco, 12AX7 q mult/af1, 6BA6 if1, 6AZ8
if2/bfo, 6BJ7 det/anl/avc, 6BZ6 calib,
6AQ5 af out, OB2 vr, 5U4 rect AF OUT:
1 W. REMARKS: Changes from HQ-110: accessory socket, 2 meter dial calibrations,
separate 6 meter coax input.

MODEL: HQ-100A YRS: 1961-64 PRICE: $189
BANDS: 4, .54-30 mHz IF: 455 kHz FILTER:
Q multiplier TUBES: 10, 6BZ6 rf, 6BE6 mix,
6C4 hfo, 2 6BA6 if, 6BV8 det/anl/bfo,
12AX7 af1/q mult, 6AQ5 af out, OB2 vr,
5Y3 rect REMARKS: Changes from HQ-100:
6BV8 replaces 6AL5 for separate BFO and
Q multiplier functions, CB channel markings on dial.

MODEL: HQ-100C REMARKS: HQ-100 with
clock.

MODEL: HQ-110AC REMARKS: HQ-110A with
clock.

MODEL: HQ-110AE REMARKS: Export model
HQ-110A for 115/230 V., 50/60 Hz.

MODEL: HQ-105TR YRS: 1961 PRICE: $219.50
REMARKS: HQ-100A with built-in CB
transmitter.

MODEL: HQ-110A-VHF YRS: 1965-69
PRICE: $299.95 BANDS: 8 Ham Bands, 160-
2 mtrs REMARKS: HQ-110A with built-in
6 and 2 meter converters using 4 nu-
vistors.

| HAMMARLUND

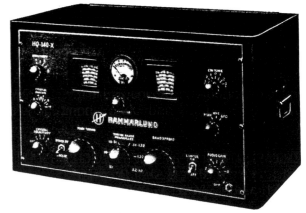

MODEL: HQ-120 YRS: 1938-44 PRICE: $117
(w/o crystal) BANDS: 6, .54-31 mHz IF: 465
kHz FILTER: Optional crystal TUBES: 12,
6S7 rf, 6K8 conv, 2 6S7 if, 6F6 if, 6H6
det/avc, 6H6 nl, 6J7 bfo, 6SF5 mtr amp,
6V6 af out, VR-150 vr, 5Z4 rect

MODEL: HQ-120X PRICE: $129 FILTER:
Crystal REMARKS: HQ-120 with crystal
filter.

MODEL: HQ-120 (Special) REMARKS: Special
model finished in black vs. the regular
gray.

MODEL: HQ-140-X YRS: 1953-55 PRICE:
$264.50 BANDS: 6, .54-31 mHz IF: 455 kHz
FILTER: Crystal TUBES: 11, 6BA6 rf, 6BE6
mix, 6C4 hfo, 3 6BA6 if, 6AL5 det/avc/anl,
12AU7 af1/bfo, 6V6 af out, VR-105/0C3
vr, 5U4 rect AF OUT: 2 W. REMARKS:
Successor to HQ-129-X. Has separate mixer and hfo, miniature tubes, other imp-
rovements.

MODEL: HQ-140-XA YRS: 1956-58 PRICE:
$249 BANDS: 6, .54-30 mHz IF: 455 kHz
FILTER: Crystal AF OUT: 2 W. REMARKS:
Improved sensitivity and more rugged
dial.

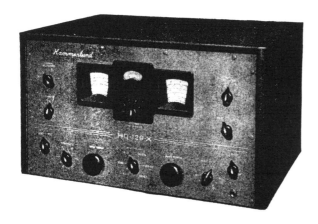

MODEL: HQ-129-X YRS: 1945-53 PRICE:
$129 ($239 in '53) BANDS: 6, .54-31 mHz
IF: 455 kHz FILTER: Crystal TUBES: 11,
6SS7 rf, 6K8 conv, 3 6SS7 if, 6H6 det/avc/
anl, 6SJ7 bfo, 6SN7 af1/meter amp, 6V6
af out, VR-105/0C3 vr, 5U4 rect AF OUT: 3
W. REMARKS: Announced 1945, first delivery 1946, successor to HQ-120.

MODEL: HQ-145 YRS: 1959-61 PRICE: $269
BANDS: 4, .54-30 mHz TYPE: Double conversion, tunable hfo IF: 3035, 455 kHz
FILTER: Crystal, slot filter TUBES: 12,
6BZ6 rf, 6BE6 mix, 6C4 hfo, 6BE6 mix2/xco,
2 6BA6 if, 6AL5 det/avc/anl, 12AX7 af1/
bfo, 6AQ5 af out, 6BZ6 calib, 0B2 vr, 5U4
rect AF OUT: 1 W.

HAMMARLUND

MODEL: HQ-145A YRS: 1964-69 REMARKS: Changes from HQ-145X: product detector, 110/230 V., 50/60 Hz power supply, "flip top" lid, silicon rectifier, accessory socket, systems socket for optional operation with HX-50, 3.2 and 500 ohm audio output, chassis cutout for coaxial antenna connector.

MODEL: HQ-145AX REMARKS: HQ-145A with 11 crystal positions for fixed frequency operation.

MODEL: HQ-145X YRS: 1961-64 PRICE: $269 BANDS: 4, .54-30 mHz TYPE: Double conversion IF: 3035, 455 kHz FILTER: Crystal, slot filter TUBES: 11, 6BZ6 rf, 6BE6 mix, 6C4 hfo, 6BE6 mix2/xco, 6AL5 det/avc/anl, 2 6BA6 if, 12AX7 af1/bfo, 6AQ5 af out, 0B2 vr, 5U4 rect AF OUT: 1 W. REMARKS: Adds one crystal controlled channel, CB channel markings on dial.

MODEL: HQ-145XC REMARKS: HQ-145X with clock.

MODEL: HQ-145XE REMARKS: Export model of HQ-145X with 115/230 V., 50/60 Hz power supply.

MODEL: HQ-145C REMARKS: HQ-145 with clock.

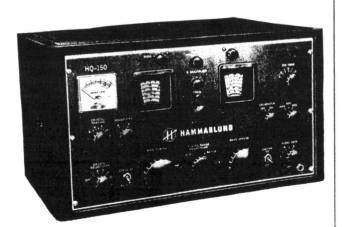

MODEL: HQ-150 YRS: 1956-58 PRICE: $294 BANDS: 6, .54-30 mHz IF: 455 kHz FILTER: Crystal and Q Multiplier TUBES: 13, 6BA6 rf, 6BE6 mix, 6C4 hfo, 3 6BA6 if, 6AL5 det/anl/avc, 12AX7 af1/bfo,

HAMMARLUND

12AX7 Q mult, 6BZ6 calib, 6V6 af out, VR-105/0C3 vr, 5U4 rect AF OUT: 2 W. REMARKS: Successor to HQ-120, HQ-129X and HQ-140.

MODEL: HQ-160 YRS: 1958-59 PRICE: $379 BANDS: 6, .54-31 mHz TYPE: Double conversion, tunable hfo IF: 3035, 455 kHz FILTER: Q multiplier TUBES: 13, 6BA6 rf, 6BE6 mix1, 6C4 hfo, 6BE6 mix2/xco, 2 6BA6 if, 6BJ7 det/nl/avc, 12AX7 af1/q mult, 6U8 prod det/bfo, 6BZ6 calib, 6AQ5 af out, 0B2 vr, 5U4 rect AF OUT: 1 W.

MODEL: HQ-170 YRS: 1958-62 PRICE: $359 BANDS: 7, 160-6 mtr ham bands TYPE: Triple conversion IF: 3035, 455, 60 kHz FILTER: 60 kHz L/C TUBES: 17, 6BZ6 rf, 6BE6 mix1, 6C4 hfo, 6BE6 mix2/xco, 6BA6 if1, 6BE6 mix3/var osc, 2 6BA6 if2/if3, 6BV8 if4/det/avc, 12AU7 prod det, 6AL5

nl, 12AU7 bfo/mtr amp, 6AV6 af1/avc clamp, 6BZ6 calib, 6AQ5 af out, 0B2 vr, 5U4 rect, AF OUT: 1 W.

MODEL: HQ-170C REMARKS: HQ-170 with clock.

MODEL: HQ-170A YRS: 1962-68 PRICE: $369 REMARKS: Changes from HQ-170; silicon rectifier, 2 meter dial scale, accessory socket, socket for transmitter/recei-ver control, "flip open" lid, hfo/mix1 on continuously.

MODEL: HQ-170ARC REMARKS: HQ-170A for rack mounting, with clock.

MODEL: HQ-170A-VHF YRS: 1964-67 PRICE: $419.95 BANDS: 8, 160-2 mtr ham bands TUBES: 20 REMARKS: Built-in 6 and 2 mtr converters using 4 nuvistors.

MODEL: HQ-180 YRS: 1959-62 PRICE: $429 BANDS: 6, .54-30 mHz TYPE: Triple con-version IF: 3035, 455, 60 kHz FILTER: 3035 kHz crystal, 60 kHz L/C TUBES: 18, 6BZ6 rf, 6BE6 mix1, 6C4 hfo, 6BE6 mix2/xco, 6BA6 if gate, 6BA6 if1, 6BE6 mix3/var osc, 2 6BA6 if, 6BV8 if4/det/avc, 12AU7 prod det, 6AL5 anl, 12AU7 bfos/meter amp, 6BZ6 calib, 6AV6 af1/avc, 6AQ5 af out, 0A2 vr, 5U4 rect AF OUT: 1 W.

MODEL: HQ-180C REMARKS: HQ-180 with clock.

MODEL: HQ-180RC REMARKS: Rack mounted

HQ-180 with clock.

MODEL: HQ-180A YRS: 1963-72 PRICE: $439 REMARKS: Changes from HQ-180; fixed/tunable bfo, silicon rectifiers, access-ory sockets, hfo/mix1 filaments on con-tinuously.

MODEL: HQ-180AC REMARKS: HQ-180A with clock.

MODEL: HQ-180AX REMARKS: HQ-180A with 11 crystal controlled fixed frequencies.

MODEL: HQ-180XE PRICE: $499.50 REM-ARKS: HQ-180 with 11 crystal controlled fixed channels and export power supply 115/230 V., 50/60 Hz.

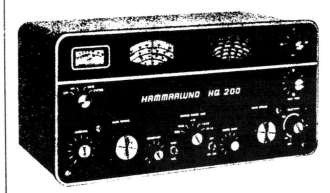

MODEL: HQ-200 YRS: 1969-72 PRICE: $229.50 BANDS: 5, .54-30 mHz FILTER: q mult TUBES: 8 + 5 semi diodes, 6BZ6 rf, 6BE6 mix, 6C4 hfo, 2 6BA6 if, 12AX7 af1/q mult, 6BE6 prod det/bfo, 6AQ5 af out, 1N34A am det, zener diode, 2 CER72C rect, 1N541A nl, AF OUT: 2.5 W.

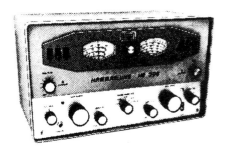

MODEL: HQ-205 YRS: 1967-69 PRICE: $259 BANDS: .54-30 mHz REMARKS: Includes a CB/10 meter transceiver with 6 crystal controlled channels.

HAMMARLUND

MODEL: PRO-310 YRS: 1955-57 PRICE: $495 BANDS: 6, .55-32.5 TYPE: Double conversion IF: 1802, 52 kHz FILTER: 52 kHz L/C TUBES: 13, 6BA6 rf, 6BE6 mix, 6C4 hfo, 6BE6 mix2/xco, 2 6BZ6 if, 6AL5 det/avc, 6AN8 bfo/buff, 12AX7 af1/anl, 6V6 af out, 6AL5 bias rect, 0B2 vr, 5U4 rect REMARKS: Turret band switch. Only one production run of 1000 receivers.

MODEL: SP-10 Super Pro (Prototype) YRS: 1935 PRICE: $182.28 BANDS: 5, .54-20 mHz IF: 465 kHz FILTER: Crystal TUBES: 15, 2 6D6 rf, 6A7 mix, 6C6 hfo, 3 6D6 if, 6B7 if/det, 6B7 avc amp, 6C6 bfo, 42 af1, 2 42 af out, 5Z3 rect, 1V bias rect AF OUT: 18 W. REMARKS: Separate power supply.

HAMMARLUND

MODEL: Super Pro SP-10 YRS: 1936 PRICE: $194 BANDS: 5, .54-20 mHz IF: 465 kHz FILTER: Crystal (Optional) TUBES: 16, 2 6D6 rf, 6A7 mix, 6C6 hfo, 3 6D6 if, 6B7 if/det, 6C6 bfo, 6B7 avc amp, 76 af1, 42 af2, 2 42 p/p af out, 1-V rect, 5Z3 rect REMARKS: Separate power supply. Originally Comet Super Pro. Separate RF and IF gain controls.

MODEL: Super Pro SP-10X PRICE: $211.68 FILTER: Crystal REMARKS: SP-10 with crystal filter.

MODEL: Super Pro SP-110 YRS: 1937-38 PRICE: $238.14 BANDS: 5, .54-20 mHz IF: 465 kHz FILTER: None TUBES: 16, 2 6K7 rf, 6L7 mix, 6J7 hfo, 3 6D6 if, 6B7 det, 6C6 bfo, 6B7 avc, 6C5 af1, 6F6 af2, 2 6F6 p/p af out, 2 rect AF OUT: 10 W. REMARKS: Variable coupling IF transformers for 3-16 kHz bandwidths, 0-2500 kHz calibrated BFO. RF and IF gain controls combined in sensitivity control.

MODEL: Super Pro SP-110LF BANDS: 0.1-20 mHz REMARKS: Broadcast band replaced with low frequency band.

MODEL: Super Pro SP-110X FILTER; Crystal REMARKS: SP-110 with crystal filter.

MODEL: Super Pro SP-110S BANDS: 5, 1.25-40 mHz REMARKS: SP-110 with special tuning range.

MODEL: Super Pro SP-110SX FILTER: Crystal REMARKS: SP-110S with crystal filter.

HAMMARLUND

MODEL: SP-120X REMARKS: SP-110X with 12" high fidelity speaker.

MODEL: SP-120SX REMARKS: SP-110SX with 12" high fidelity speaker.

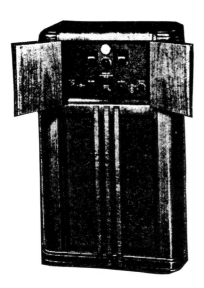

MODEL: Super Pro SP-150 REMARKS: Console model of SP-110. Walnut finished panel, brown bakelite knobs, gold-filled engraved labels, bronze tuning meter case, brass band switch scale. Console contains 15" bass reflex speaker. Simplified operation with elimination of send-receive switch, speaker phones switch, BFO pitch control, off-on switch (added to audio gain control). Added phone jack to front panel.

MODEL: SP-150S BANDS: 5, 1.25-40 mHz REMARKS: SP-150 with special tuning range.

MODEL: SP-210SX BANDS: 5, 1.25-40 mHz REMARKS: Same as SP-210X except for tuning range.

MODEL: SP-210X YRS: 1939-45 PRICE: $279 BANDS: 5, .54-20 mHz IF: 465 kHz FILTER: Crystal TUBES: 18, 2 6K7 rf, 6L7 mix, 6J7 hfo, 6K7 if1, 2 6SK7 if2/3, 6H6 det, 6N7 nl, 6SJ7 bfo, 6SK7 avc amp, 6H6 mtr rect/ avc rect, 6C5 af1, 6F6 af2, 2 6F6 p/p af out, 5Z3 rect, 80 rect AF OUT: 16 W. REMARKS: Separate power supply, supplied with 10" speaker.

MODEL: SP-210 LX BANDS: 0.1-20 mHz REMARKS: Broadcast band replaced with low frequency band.

MODEL: SP-220SX REMARKS: SP-210SX with 12" speaker.

MODEL: SP-220X REMARKS: SP-210X with 12" speaker.

MODEL: SPC-400X YRS: 1946-47 PRICE: $342 BANDS: 5, .54-30 mHz IF: 455 kHz FILTER: Crystal TUBES: 18, 2 6K7 rf, 6L7 mix, 6J7 hfo, 6K7 if1, 2 6SK7 if2/3, 6H6 det, 6N7 nl, 6SJ7 bfo, 6SK7 avc amp, 6H6 avc rect, 6J5 af1, 6F6 af2, 2 6V6 p/p af out, 5Y3 bias rect, 5U4 hv rect AF OUT: 8 W. REMARKS: Separate power supply, cabinet model.

MODEL: SPR-400X REMARKS: Rack mounted model.

HAMMARLUND

MODEL: SPC-400SX BANDS: 5, 1.25-40 mHz
REMARKS: SPC-400X with special tuning
range.

MODEL: SP-600 (Generic Model) YEARS:
1950-72 PRICE: $985 BANDS: 6, .54-54 mHz
TYPE: Double Conv. IF: 3955, 455 kHz
FILTER: Crystal TUBES: 20, 2 6BA6 rf,
6BE6 mix 1, 6C4 hfo, 6BA6 gate, 6BE6 mix
2, 6C4 xco, 3 6BA6 if, 12AU7 if K fol/
af1, 6AL5 det/avc, 6C4 bfo, 6BA6 buff,
6AL5 anl/mtr rect, 6AC7 xco, 6V6 af out,
6AL5 bias rect, 5R4 rect, 0A2 vr AF OUT:
2.5 W. REMARKS: 10,000 produced by 1953,
turret coil switching, military designation
R-274.
MODEL: SP-600J REMARKS: "J" indicates JAN
level construction and components.

MODEL: SP-600JLX PRICE: $1260 BANDS: 6,
0.1-0.4, 1.35-29.7 mHz REMARKS: Low frequency SP-600JX.

MODEL: SP-600JX REMARKS: JAN level receiver with six crystal controlled channels.

MODEL: SP-600JX-17 REMARKS: Special diversity model of SP-600JX with provisions
for master or slave operation.

MODEL: SP-600JX-21 REMARKS: Details not
known.

MODEL: SP-600JX-21A YRS: 1970-72 PRICE:
$1595 BANDS: 6, .54-54 mHz REMARKS:
Other details not known.

MODEL: SP-600JX-26 BANDS: 6, .54-54 mHz
REMARKS: Other details not known.

MODEL: SP-600VLF PRICE: $1975 (1956)
BANDS: 6, .01-.54 mHz REMARKS: VLF version of SP-600. Has six crystal controlled
channels.

MODEL: SP-600X REMARKS: "X" indicates
the model includes six crystal controlled
channels.

MODEL: SPC-600-X (Prototype) YEARS:
1948 PRICE: $395 BANDS: 6, .54-54 mHz
FILTER: Crystal TUBES: 19, 3 6BA6, 2
6BE6, 2 6C4, 6J5, 4 6SG7, 6SN7, 2 6H6, 2
6V6, 5U4, VR150 REMARKS: Differs in appearance and tubes from SP-600, probably
a prototype that was never delivered.

MODEL: AACS BANDS: 0.3-10 mHz REMARKS:
Military version of Super Pro.

HAMMARLUND

MODEL: BC-779 YRS: 1942-46 BANDS: 5, 0.1-0.4, 2.5-20 mHz IF: 465 kHz FILTER: Crystal TUBES: 16 REMARKS: Military SP-200, separate power supply.

MODEL: BC-779A REMARKS: See BC-779

MODEL: BC-779B REMARKS: See BC-779.

MODEL: BC-779/129-U BANDS: 5, 0.3-10 mHz

MODEL: BC-789 REMARKS: Military Sp-400.

MODEL: BC-794 YRS: 1942-46 BANDS: 5, 1.25-40 mHz IF: 465 kHz FILTER: Crystal TUBES: 16 REMARKS: Military SP-200, separate power supply. Same as BC-779 except frequency coverage.

MODEL: BC-796 REMARKS: Super Pro.

MODEL: BC-799/A/B/C REMARKS: Super Pro.

MODEL: BC-1004/A/B/C/D BANDS: 5, .54-20 mHz REMARKS: Same as BC-779 except for frequency coverage.

MODEL: R-129/U REMARKS: Same as BC-779/129-U, qv.

MODEL: R-270 REMARKS: BC-794

MODEL: R-274C/FRR REMARKS: SP-600

MODEL: R-320A REMARKS: SP-600JX Diversity.

MODEL: R-483 REMARKS: SP-600 (R-274A), part of SCR-244D

MODEL: R-542 REMARKS: SP-600.

MODEL: RBG-2 YRS: 1943 BANDS: 6, .54-31, calibrated bandspread 4-4.6, 8-9.6, 12-13.6, 15-18 mHz IF: 455 kHz FILTER: Crystal TUBES: 11, 6SK7 rf, 6K8 conv, 3 6SK7 if, 6H6 det/avc/nl, 6C5 af1, 6SJ7 bfo, 6V6 af out, VR105 vr, 5U4 rect REMARKS: Navy receiver type CHC-46140. Appears to be early HQ-129.

MODEL: RGB REMARKS: Manufactured for the Navy.

HARVEY-WELLS

Cliff Harvey, W1RE, and John Wells, W1ZD, formed Harvey-Wells Electronics in 1939. Harvey had previously owned Harvey Radio, started in 1936. Harvey-Wells manufactured police radios, transceivers, transmitters and crystals. Perhaps their best known product was the TBS-50 Bandmaster transmitter.

MODEL: R-9 YRS: 1954-56 PRICE: $149.50 BANDS: 5, 10-80 mtrs TYPE: Double conversion, variable hfo IF: 1600, 260 kHz FILTER: Optional crystal TUBES: 10, 6BJ6 rf, 6U8 mix1/hfo, 6U8 mix2/xco, 2 6BJ6 if, 6AL5 det/nl, 12AX7 af1/bfo, 6CM6 af out, 0A2 vr, 5Y3 rect AF OUT: 5 W. REMARKS: Internal 115 V. power supply, can be powered by external 6/12 V. vibrator or dynamotor power supply.

MODEL: R-9A YRS: 1958 PRICE: $149.50 BANDS: 5 ham bands, 10-80 mtrs TYPE: Double conversion, variable hfo IF: 1600, 260 kHz TUBES: 10

HEATH

Edward Heath started the Heath Co, Benton Harbor, MI, after World War II. The first product was a 5 inch oscilloscope kit using mostly war surplus components. The product line rapidly expanded to include additional test equipment and amateur equipment in kit form. The AR-1, 1950, was the first of a line of receiver kits.

HEATH

MODEL: AR-1 YRS: 1950-53 PRICE: $23.50
BANDS: 3, .55-20 mHz IF: 455 kHz FILTER:
None TUBES: 6, including 12SH7 mix, 1626
hfo, 12SH7 if, 12J5 bfo AF OUT: 3 W.
REMARKS: Kit, BC type receiver, no BFO.
bandspread, phone jack or AVC switch.

MODEL: AR-2 YRS: 1953-56 PRICE: $25.50
BANDS: 4, .55-35 mHz IF: 455 kHz FILTER:
None TUBES: 6, 12BE6 conv, 12BA6 if,
12AV6 det/avc/af1, 12BA6 bfo, 12A6 af
out, 5Y3 rect REMARKS: Kit, internal
speaker.

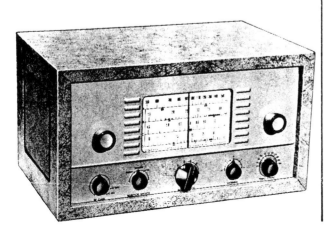

HEATH

MODEL: AR-3 YRS: 1956-60 PRICE: $29.95
BANDS: 4, .55-30 mHz IF: 455 kHz FILTER:
None TUBES: 6, 12BE6 conv, 12BA6 if,
12AV6 det/avc/af1, 12BA6 bfo, 12A6 af
out, 5Y3 rect REMARKS: Kit, internal
speaker. New high Q slug tuned coils,
new layout, new type IF transformers.

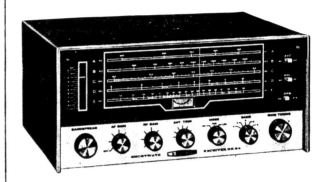

MODEL: GR-54 YRS: 1966-68 PRICE: $84.95
BANDS: 5, .18-.42, .54-30 mHz IF: 1682 kHz
FILTER: None TUBES: 6 + 8 semi diodes,
6BH6 rf, 6EA8 mix/hfo, 2 6BA6 if, 12AT7
prod det/bfo, 6HF8 af1/af out, 8 diodes
avc/det/anl/rect REMARKS: Kit.

MODEL: GR-64 YRS: 1966-68 PRICE: $39.95
BANDS: 4, .55-30 mHz FILTER: None TUBES:
4 + 2 Si rect REMARKS: Kit, internal
speaker.

MODEL: GR-91 YRS: 1961 PRICE: $39.95
BANDS: 4, .55-30 mHz IF: 455 kHz FILTER:
None TUBES: 4 + rect REMARKS: Internal
speaker.

MODEL: HR-10 YRS: 1963-66 PRICE: $79.95
BANDS: 5 ham bands, 80-10 mtrs IF: 1680
kHz FILTER: Crystal lattice TUBES: 7,
6BZ6 rf, 6EA8 mix/hfo, 6BA6 if, 6EA8 if/
bfo, 6BJ7 det/avc/anl, 6EA8 af1/af out,
6X4 rect REMARKS: Kit.

MODEL: HR-10B YRS: 1967-68 PRICE: $75
BANDS: 5 ham bands, 80-10 mtrs REMARKS:
Kit.

MODEL: MR-1 Comanche YRS: 1959-60 PRICE:
$119.95 BANDS: 5 ham bands, 80-10 mtrs
IF: 3000 kHz FILTER: Crystal lattice
TUBES: 8, 6BZ6 rf, 6EA8 mix/hfo, 6BZ6 if1,
6EA8 if2/mtr amp, 6T8 det/agc/nl/af1,
6BE6 prod det/bfo, 6AQ5 af out, 0A2 vr
REMARKS: Kit. Separate power supply.

MODEL: RX-1 Mohawk YRS: 1958-63 PRICE:
$274.95 BANDS: 7 ham bands, 160-10 mtrs
TYPE: Double conversion, variable hfo
IF: 1682, 50 kHz FILTER: 50 kHz L/C
TUBES: 15, 6BZ6 rf, 6CS6 mix1, 12AT7 hfo/
k fol, 6BA6 if, 6BE6 mix2, 12AT7 xco,
2 6BA6 if, 6BJ7 det/anl/avc, 6CS6 prod
det/bfo, 12AT7 af1/mtr amp, 6AQ5 af
out, 6BA6 calib, 0A2 vr, 5V4 rect AF OUT:
2 W. REMARKS: Kit.

MODEL: HR-20 YRS: 1962-64 PRICE: $134-50
BANDS: 5 ham bands, 80-10 mtrs IF:
3000 kHz FILTER: Crystal lattice TUBES: 8,
6BZ6 rf, 6EA8 mix/hfo, 6BZ6 if1, 6BZ6 if2/
mtr amp, 6BJ7 det/avc/nl, 6BE6 prod det/
bfo, 6EB8 af1/af out, 0A2 vr REMARKS:
Kit. Separate power supply.

HEATH

MODEL: SB-300 YRS: 1963-66 PRICE: $264.95
BANDS: 8 500 kHz bands, 80-10 mtrs
TYPE: Double conversion, fixed hfo IF:
8400-8900, 3395 kHz FILTER: crystal lattice TUBES: 10 + 6 semi diodes, 6BZ6 rf,
6AU6 mix1, 6AB4 xco, 6AU6 mix2, 6AU6
vfo, 2 6BA6 if, 6AS11 prod det/bfo/k fol,
6HF8 af1/af out, 6AU6 calib, CR3 det,
2 CR avc, 3 CR rect REMARKS: Kit.

MODEL: SB-301 YRS: 1966-69 PRICE: $260
BANDS: 9 500 kHz bands, 80-10 mtrs +
WWV TYPE: Double conversion, fixed hfo
IF: 8395-8895, 3395 kHz FILTER: Crystal
lattice TUBES: 10 + 8 semi diodes, 6BZ6 rf,
6AU6 mix1, 6AB4 xco, 6AU6 mix2, 6AU6 lmo,
2 6BA6 if, 6AS11 prod det/bfo/bfo amp,
6HF8 af1/af out, 6AU6 calib, CR det, 2 CR
avc, 2 CR anl, 3 CR rect AF OUT: 1 W. RE-
MARKS: Kit. Changes from SB-300: RTTY
position, 15-15.5 mHz range, switched anl,
provision for 6 and 2 meter converters.

MODEL: SB-310 YRS: 1967-68 PRICE: $280
BANDS: 9 500 kHz bands, 3.5-30 mHz
TYPE: Double conversion, fixed hfo IF:
8395-8895, 3395 kHz FILTER: Crystal lattice TUBES: 10 + 8 semi diodes, 6BZ6 rf,
6AU6 mix1, 6AB4 xco, 6AU6 mix2, 6CB6

HEATH

vfo, 2 6BA6 if, 6AV11 prod det/bfo/af k
fol, 6HF8 af1/af out, 6AU6 calib, 1N91
det, 2 1N458 agc, 2 S187 nl, 3 1N2079
rect AF OUT: 1 W. REMARKS: Kit. SWL version of SB-301.

HENDRICKS & HARVEY

Hendricks & Harvey was located at
408 Main Street, Hartford, Conn. They
advertised a "built to order" single signal receiver in late 1932 and early 1933,
shortly after James Lamb's articles on
the crystal filter.

MODEL: Variation 1 YRS: 1932-33 PRICE:
$225 BANDS: 4 FILTER: Crystal TUBES:
8 REMARKS: "Built to order." Separate
power supply, plug-in coils.

MODEL: Variation 2 YRS: 1933 PRICE: $225
BANDS: 4 FILTER: Crystal TUBES: 9 including 1 rf, 2 if, det, bfo, 59 af out RE-
MARKS: "Individually custom built." Plug-in coils, separate power supply. Has agc.

HOWARD

The Howard Radio Company of Belmont Avenue in Chicago was a long time
manufacturer of broadcast receivers.
From 1938 to 1942 Howard offered a full
line of communications receivers. They
had a full page advertisement in the
1946 ARRL Handbook promoting a postwar line of quality receivers but were
never heard from again. We believe they
never did produce a postwar receiver.

MODEL: 435-A YRS: 1941-42 PRICE: $36.75
BANDS: 4, .55-43 mHz IF: 465 kHz FILTER:
None TUBES: 7, 6SD7 rf, 6SA7 conv, 6SK7
if, 6SQ7 det/avc/af1, 6J5 bfo, 6K8 af out,
5Y3 rect REMARKS: Internal speaker.
Optional transformer for 110/117/140/
230 V., 40 Hz and optional "S" meter.

MODEL: 430 YRS: 1938 PRICE: $29.95 BANDS:
4, .54-40 mHz IF: 465 kHz FILTER: None
TUBES: 6, 6K8 conv, 6K7 if, 6Q7 det/af1/
avc, 6C5 bfo, 41 af out, 5W4 rect AF OUT:
2.5 W.

MODEL: 430 - Type 2 YRS: 1938-39 PRICE:
$29.95 REMARKS: Same as previous model
except has auxilliary socket for battery
power supply and external "R" meter.

MODEL: 436 YRS: 1939-40 PRICE: $39.95
BANDS: 4, .54-43 mHz IF: 465 kHz FILTER:
None TUBES: 7, 6K8 conv, 6SK7 if, 6SQ7
det/af1, 6C5 bfo, 6H6 nl, 6K6 af out, 80
rect

MODEL: 436-A YRS: 1941-42 PRICE: $41.75
BANDS: 4, .54-43 mHz IF: 465 kHz FILTER:
None TUBES: 8, 6SD7 rf, 6SA7 conv, 6SK7
if, 6SQ7 det/avc/af1, 6J5 bfo, 6K6 af
out, 6H6 nl, 5Y3 rect REMARKS: Internal
speaker. Adds noise limiter to 435-A.
Optional "S" meter available.

MODEL: 435 YRS: 1940-41 PRICE: $29.95
BANDS: 4, .54-40 mHz IF: 465 kHz FILTER:
None TUBES: 6, 6K8 conv, 6SK7 if, 6Q7
det/af1, 6K6 af out, 5W4 rect AF OUT:
2.5 W. REMARKS: Internal speaker.

HOWARD

MODEL: 437 YRS: 1940 PRICE: $54.50, $62.50 with crystal BANDS: 4, .54-43 mHz IF: 465 kHz FILTER: Crystal (Optional) TUBES: 9, including 1 rf, 2 if stages.

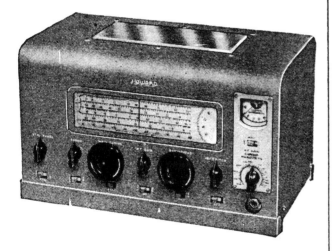

MODEL: 437-A YRS: 1941-42 PRICE: $61.95, $69.75 with crystal, $85.50 with meter BANDS: 4, .54-43 mHz IF: 465 kHz FILTER: Crystal (optional) TUBES: 9 REMARKS: Optional crystal and "S" meter.

HOWARD

HOWARD: 438 YRS: 1939 PRICE: $49.95 (less crystal) BANDS: 4, .54-43 mHz IF: 465 kHz FILTER: Crystal (optional) TUBES: 8, 6K7 rf, 6K8 conv, 2 6K7 if, 6Q7 det/avc/af1, 6C5 bfo, 41 af out, 80 rect AF OUT: 2 W. REMARKS: Internal speaker. Optional crystal and "S" meter.

MODEL: 440 YRS: 1938-39 PRICE: $74.45, $84.45 with crystal BANDS: 5, .54-40 mHz IF: 465 kHz FILTER: Crystal (Optional) TUBES: 9, 6K7 rf, 6K8 conv, 2 6K7 if, 6Q7 det/avc/af1, 6J7 bfo, 6J5 mtr amp, 6V6 af out, 80 rect

MODEL: 445 YRS: 1941-42 PRICE: $36.75 BANDS: 4, .55-43 mHz IF: 465 kHz FILTER: None TUBES: 6 REMARKS: Internal speaker. AC/DC power supply. Same as 435-A except AC/DC.

MODEL: 450 YRS: 1938 BANDS: 6, .54-65 mHz IF: 1560 kHz band 6, 465 kHz bands 1-5 TUBES: 12 AF OUT: 8 W. REMARKS: RF amplifier not used on band 6. Weighs 50 lbs.

HOWARD

MODEL: 450-A YRS: 1938-39 PRICE: $95.45,
$105.45 with crystal BANDS: 6, .55-65 mHz
IF: 1560 kHz band 6, 465 kHz bands 1-5
FILTER: Crystal (optional) TUBES: 12, 6K7
rf, 6L7 mix, 6J6 hfo, 2 6K7 if, 6Q7 det/af1,
6J7 bfo, 6J5 meter amp, 6J5 af inv, 2 6V6
af out, 80 rect AF OUT: 9.5 W. REMARKS:
RF amplifier not used on band 6.

MODEL: 460 YRS: 1939-40 PRICE: $79.95,
$89.95 with crystal BANDS: 4, .54-43 mHz
IF: 465 kHz FILTER: Crystal (optional)
TUBES: 10, 6K6 monitor, 6SK7 rf, 6K8 conv,
6SF5 meter amp, 2 6SK7 if, 6SQ7 det/af1,
6N6 nl, 6V6 af out, 80 rect AF OUT: 4 W.
REMARKS: Built-in frequency monitor.

HOWARD

MODEL: 490 YRS: 1940-42 PRICE: $149.50
BANDS: 6, .54-30 mHz IF: 465 kHz FILTER:
Crystal TUBES: 14, 2 6AB7(1853) rf, 6SA7
mix, 6SA7 hfo, 2 6SK7 if, 6H6 det/avc/nl,
6SF5 af1, 6J5 phase inv, 6J5 bfo, 7E7
meter amp, 2 6K6 af out, 5Y3 rect AF OUT:
8 W.

ITT MACKAY MARINE

Mackay Marine is an old time manu-
of marine communications systems and
they continue in business today with a
respected line of solid state gear. They
made a number of vacuum tube communications receivers but they were not
usually available to the public. In the
1960's they did try to sell one of their
models to the amateur market.

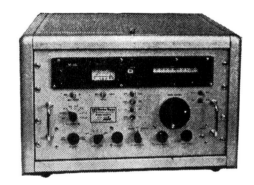

From April, 1967, QST, courtesy ARRL

MODEL: 3010-B YRS: Late 1960's PRICE:
$1600 BANDS: 15 2 mHz bands, .07-30 mHz
TYPE: Triple conversion, fixed hfo, up
conversion IF: 37-39 mHz, 5940, 455 kHz
FILTER: Mechanical TUBES: 17 + 8 semi
diodes, 7788 rf, 6C4 k fol, 4 1N82A mix1,
6BL8 xco/k fol, 6688 if, 6BL8 k fol/mix2,
6BA6 vfo, 6U8 xco/premix, 6EW6 inj amp,
6BE6 mix3/xco, 2 6BA6 if, 12AT7 prod det,
6AU6 bfo, 6AV6 det/avc/af1, 6BF5 af
out, 6BA6 calib, 0B2 vr, 2 CR anl, 2 CR
rect

JEFFERSON-TRAVIS

Jefferson-Travis Radio Manufacturing
Corp., a manufacturer of two-way radio
equipment, was located on East 23rd
Street in New York. They had a two page
advertisement in the 1945 ARRL Hand-

JEFFERSON-TRAVIS

book announcing a new general coverage receiver. Nothing more is known about this receiver.

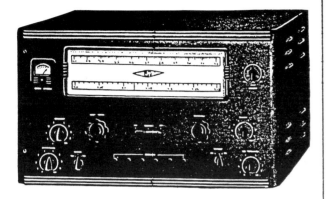

MODEL: CR-1 YRS: 1945 BANDS: 5, .54-32 mHz FILTER: Crystal TUBES: 15, includes 2 rf and p/p af out AF OUT: 10 W.

KAAR ENGINEERING

Kaar Engineering Co. was located in Palo Alto, Calif.

MODEL: KE-23A YRS: c. 1944 BANDS: 4, 0.5-42 mHz IF: 455 kHz FILTER: None TUBES: 9, 6SK7 rf, 6K8 conv, 6SK7 if, 6H6 anl, 6SQ7 det/sq/avc, 6SQ7 af1, 6SK7 bfo, 6V6 af out, 5Y3 rect REMARKS: No filter, "S" meter. Has electrical bandspread.

MODEL: KE-23AT YRS: c. 1944 REMARKS: Has universal power transformer 100/120/ 150/210/230 V., 40-60 Hz. Also includes "S" meter and mechanical bandspread.

KARADIO

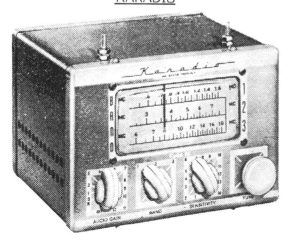

KARADIO

MODEL: 80-C YRS: 1952 BANDS: .54-17.5 mHz FILTER: None TUBES: 6, 6BA6 rf, 6BE6 conv, 6BA6 if, 6AT6 det/af1, 6AQ5 af out, 6X5 rect REMARKS: Mobile-type receiver. Separate vibrator power supply.

KNIGHT

The Knight name was used by Allied Radio (q.v.) for their house brand equipment.

LAFAYETTE

Wholesale Lafayette, a New York based distributor, began offering communications receivers in the mid-1930's and continued to offer them through the late 1970's as Lafayette Radio. Many of the post-war receivers were imported.

MODEL: Professional 9 YRS: 1935-36 PRICE: $36.75 kit, $44.25 wired BANDS: 4, .55-30 mHz IF: 470 kHz FILTER: None TUBES: 9, 6D6 rf, 6C6 mix, 41 hfo, 6D6 if, 6B7 det/avc/if2, 76 bfo, 6C6 af1, 42 af out, 80 rect REMARKS: Kit or assembled. Preassembled tuning unit, airplane dial, internal speaker.

LAFAYETTE

LAFAYETTE

MODEL: HA-225 YRS: 1966 PRICE: $129.95
BANDS: 5, .15-54 mHz TUBES: 14

MODEL: HA-230 (KT-340) YRS: 1965-66
PRICE: $74.50 kit, $89.50 wired BANDS: 4,
.55-30 mHz FILTER: Q-multiplier TUBES: 8
REMARKS: Kit or assembled. Imported.

MODEL: HA-350 YRS: 1964-67 PRICE: $189.50
BANDS: 7 600 kHz ham bands (80-10 mtrs)
plus WWV TYPE: Double conversion, fixed
hfo IF: 3500-4000, 455 kHz FILTER: Mechanical TUBES: 12 + 3 semi diodes, 6BZ6
rf, 6BL8 mix1/xco, 6BE6 mix2, 6BA6 vfo,
2 6BA6 if, 1N60 det, 6AL5 avc/anl, 6AQ8
prod det/calib, 6BA6 bfo, 6AV6 af1, 6AQ5
af out, 0B2 vr, 2 CR rect REMARKS: Imported.

MODEL: HA-500 YRS: 1966 PRICE: $149.95
BANDS: 6, 80-10 meters FILTER: Mechanical TUBES: 10

MODEL: HA-700 YRS: 1966 PRICE: $89.95
BANDS: 5, .15-.4, .55-30 mHz IF: 455 kHz
FILTER: Mechanical TUBES: 6 + 7 semi
diodes, 6BA6 rf, 6BL8 mix/hfo, 2 6BA6 if,
6AQ8 prod det/bfo, 6BM8 af1/af out, 2
1N60 avc, 1N60 det, 1N60 mtr rect, SW-05S
anl, 2 FR-1K rect AF OUT: 1.3 W.

MODEL: HE-10 (KT-200WX) YRS: 1959-63
PRICE: $64.50 kit, $79.95 assembled BANDS:
4, .55-31 mHz IF: 455 kHz FILTER: None
TUBES: 9, 6BD6 rf, 6BE6 mix, 6BE6 hfo,
2 6BD6 if, 6AV6 det/avc/af1, 6AV6 bfo/nl,
6AR5 af out, 5Y3 rect AF OUT: 1.5 W. RE-
MARKS: Kit or assembled. Imported.

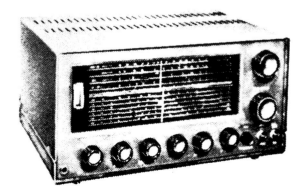

LAFAYETTE

MODEL: HE-30 (KT-320) YRS: 1961-64
PRICE: $64.95 kit, $79.95 assembled BANDS:
4, .55-30 mHz IF: 455 kHz FILTER: Q-multiplier TUBES: 9, 6BA6 rf, 6BE6 mix, 6BE6
hfo, 6AV6 q-mult/bfo, 2 6BA6 if, 6AV6 det/
anl/af1, 6AQ5 af out, 5Y3 rect AF OUT:
1.5 W. REMARKS: Imported.

MODEL: HE-40 YRS: 1961-63 PRICE: $54.50
BANDS: .55-30 mHz REMARKS: Internal
speaker.

MODEL: H-60 YRS: c. 1962 PRICE: $39.95
BANDS: 4, .55-30 mHz FILTER: None TUBES:
3 + semi diode REMARKS: Internal speaker.

MODEL: HE80WX YRS: 1963-64 PRICE: $149
BANDS: 5, .55-54 mHz TYPE: Single conversion, except dual conversion on 6 mtrs
FILTER: Q multiplier TUBES: 15 + 1 semi
diode, 6AQ8 6 mtr rf, 6AQ8 6 mtr conv,
6BA6 rf, 6BE6 mix, 6AQ8 hfo/buff, 2 6BA6
if, 6AL5 det/anl, 6BE6 prod det, 6AQ8 af1/
bfo, 6AQ5 af out, 6AQ8 q mult/calib, 6CA4
rect, 0A2 vr, 1N60 calib REMARKS: Import.

LEEDS

Leeds was a radio distributor on Ver-
sey Street in New York City.

MODEL: Supreme YRS: 1933 PRICE: $95.00
BANDS: 5, 1.5-20 mHz IF: 465 kHz FILTER:
Crystal TUBES: 9, 58 rf, 58 mix, 24A hfo,
2 58 if, 55 det/avc, 56 bfo, 247 af out,
80 rect REMARKS: Kit. Uses National ham
bandspread or general coverage coils.

LINCOLN

Lincoln Radio Corp., Chicago, was a
manufacturer of high-end, custom
broadcast receivers that competed with
E. H. Scott and McMurdo Silver. William
H. Hollister was president and chief
engineer. Hollister was also a ham and
in 1933 introduced the R-9, one of the
early communications receivers.

MODEL: CQ YRS: 1934-35 BANDS: 5 TUBES:
8, including 1 rf, 2 if REMARKS: Kit.

LINCOLN

MODEL: R-9 YRS: 1933 BANDS: 5, 1.5-33
mHz IF: 175 kHz FILTER: None TUBES: 11,
58 mix, 56 hfo, 3 58 if, 6P Wunderlich
det/avc, 56 af1, 56 bfo, 2 45 p/p af
out, 80 rect REMARKS: Tuning meter,
separate power supply.

McCULLA MFG

In 1934 McCulla Mfg Co, Waukegan, IL,
(formerly National Pfanstiehl Radio Corp)
manufactured and advertised the "Pfanstiehl Single Side Band Superheterodyne
Communication Receiver."

MODEL: 70A/X Pfanstiehl Super YRS: 1934
PRICE: $34.95, $46.71 w/xtal BANDS: 6,
1.05-21 mHz FILTER: Crystal (optional)
TUBES: 8, 57 mix, 58 bfo, 2 58 if, 2B7 det/
avc/af1, 58 bfo, 59 af out AF OUT: 3 W.
REMARKS: Plug-in coils, separate power
supply with 80 rect. Supplied with 4 sets
of coils for 20, 40, 80, 160 mtrs. Air tuned
IF transformers optional extra.

McCULLA MFG

MODEL: 70AB/X TUBES: 7, 77 mix, 78 hfo,
2 78 if, 6B7 det/avc/af1, 78 bfo, 41 af out
REMARKS: Battery version of 70A.

MCMURDO SILVER INC

McMurdo Silver started his first company, Silver-Marshall, in 1924 at the age of
21. The original location was a 1600 sq.
ft. loft over a garage in Evanston, IL.
By 1929 S-M moved into a 106,000 sq. ft.
plant at 6401 W. 65th St., Chicago. They
manufactured components, audio transformers, variable capacitors, coils,
sockets, dials, speakers, and by 1928
claimed 10% of the U. S. parts business. In
addition, S-M manufactured a line of home
BC receivers and a number of all-wave
regenerative receivers.

Silver-Marshall declared bankruptcy
in October, 1932, during the depths of the
depression and Silver immediately formed
a new company, McMurdo Silver, Inc., to
manufacture custom, all-wave receivers
which competed at the top of the line
with E. H. Scott and Lincoln Radio.

The firm started at 1136 W. Austin
Ave, Chicago, moved to 1747 Belmont St
in 1933, to 3358 N. Paulina St in 1934 and,
finally, to 2900 S. Michigan Blvd in 1936.
Silver manufactured his own sets until a
suit by RCA halted production in 1934.
Howard Radio (q.v.) manufactured the
Silver receivers from April, 1934, to late
1935 when Silver received an RCA license
and resumed production.

The mainstay of the Silver line was the
Masterpiece receiver which was updated
annually which culminated in 1937 with the
Masterpiece VI. The advertising for the
receivers was as gaudy as the chrome
plated sets themselves. In 1937 as E. H.
Scott was proclaiming his 31 tube Philharmonic XXX to be the "World's Most
Powerful Radio" Silver touted the Masterpiece VI as the "Finest Receiver Ever
Built."

McMurdo Silver was a prolific writer
who promoted his products by authoring
dozens of articles in the radio magazines

MCMURDO SILVER INC

of the 1920's, 1930's and 1940's. As an advertising promotion Admiral Byrd carried a Masterpiece II on his 1933-34 Antarctic expedition. Another widely advertised promotion was a DX listening contest in Hollywood between Bing Crosby and Richard Arlen, each using a Masterpiece III, in late 1934.

The company became the McMurdo Silver Corp., Division of GPH, Inc, in May, 1935, with the purchase of a controlling interest in the company by Glen's Patents & Holdings of England. Silver became chief engineer.

McMurdo Silver, Inc, closed its doors in 1938 due to poor sales. Its assets were purchased by rival E. H. Scott in November, 1938. A British offshoot, British McMurdo Silver, Ltd, continued on into 1939 before closing down also. Silver moved on to E. I. Guthman (q.v.) as an engineer and designed a unique receiver and a line of ham accessories. After Guthman closed their equipment line in 1940 Silver spent the war years working for Lear, Fada and Grenby Mfg. In 1945 he formed his last company, McMurdo Silver Co, Inc, (q.v.) in Hartford, CT, to manufacture a line of test equipment and some simple ham gear. McMurdo Silver died in 1948 at the age of 45.

MODEL: 3A Ham Super YRS: 1933 BANDS: 4, 1.5-10 mHz TUBES: 7 REMARKS: Three gang plug-in coils, regeneration.

MODEL: 3A Ham Super (Variation) TUBES: 6 REMARKS: Battery operated version.

MCMURDO SILVER INC

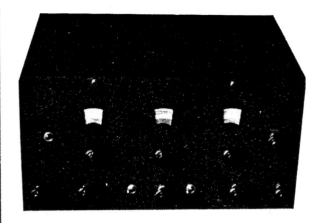

MODEL: 5A Silver Single Signal Super YRS: 1933 BANDS: 4, 1.5-25 mHz FILTER: Crystal TUBES: includes 2A7 det/agc REMARKS: Three dials, bandswitching, agc.

MODEL: 5B YRS: 1934 PRICE: $59.70 BANDS: 3, 1.55-30 mHz IF: 465 kHz FILTER: Crystal (Optional) TUBES: 8, 58 rf, 2A7 conv, 2 58 if, 56 det/af1, 58 bfo, 59 af out, 5Z3 rect AF OUT; 3 W. REMARKS: Bandswitching.

MODEL: 5C Single Signal Super YRS: 1934-35 PRICE: $74.70, $83.50 with crystal BANDS: 3, 1.5-23 mHz IF: 465 kHz FILTER: Crystal (Optional) TUBES: 8, 58 rf, 2A7 conv, 2 58 if, 55 det/avc/af1, 2A5 af out, 58 bfo, 80 rect AF OUT: 3 W.

MCMURDO SILVER INC

MODEL: 5D Radio Silver YRS: 1935-36
PRICE: $109.80 BANDS: 4, 1.7-33 mHz IF: 465
kHz FILTER: Crystal TUBES: 10, 2 6D6 rf,
6D6 mix, 76 hfo, 6D6 if amp, 6C6 det, 6B7
avc amp, 76 bfo, 42 af out, 5Z3 rect RE-
MARKS: Kit sponsored by several components manufacturers. Designed by McMurdo Silver.

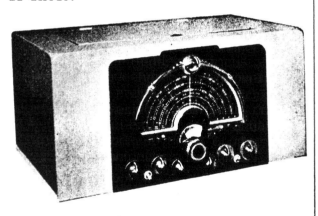

MODEL: 14-15 YRS: 1938 BANDS: 4, .54-32
mHz IF: 472 kHz FILTER: L/C TUBES: 14 or
15, 6K7 rf, 6L7 mix, 6J7 hfo, 2 6K7 if,
6J5 det, 6K7 avc amp, 6H6 avc rect/eye
rect, 6G5 eye, 6J5 bfo, 6J5 af1, 2 6L6
p/p af out, (2) 5Z3 rect AF OUT: 20 W.
REMARKS: Regenerative RF amplifier, one
5Z3 used for 10" speaker model, two 5Z3
used for 15" model.

MCMURDO SILVER INC

MODEL: Masterpiece III-X YRS: 1934-35
FILTER: Single crystal for CW, dual crystals 700 Hz apart for phone TUBES: Includes rf, 3 if stages REMARKS: Communications version of Masterpiece III. First
use of crystal lattice filter?

MODEL: Super Gainer YRS: 1935-36 PRICE:
$23.40 BANDS: 5, 10-160 mtr ham bands
IF: 465 kHz FILTER: Regen 2nd det TUBES:
3, 6C6 regen mix, 76 hfo, 79 regen det/af
REMARKS: Plug-in coils, separate power
supply.

MCMURDO SILVER CO

McMurdo Silver, Co., Inc., 1240 Main St,
Hartford, Conn., was McMurdo Silver's
last venture before his death at the age
of 45 in 1948. The company manufactured
test equipment and ham gear.

MODEL: 802 YRS: 1947-48 PRICE: $38.95 plus
tubes, power supply and coils BANDS: 6,
ham bands 80-6 mtrs IF: 735 kHz FILTER:
Regenerative IF TUBES: 5, 6BE6 conv, 6BA6
if, 6J6 det/nl, 6J6 af1/bfo, 6AK6 af out
REMARKS: Similar to ARRL Handbook design. Plug-in coils, internal speaker, separate power supply.

MEISSNER

The Meissner Manufacturing Co., located in Mt. Carmel, Ill., manufactured coils and transformers. During the later half of the 1930's they also sold various kit equipment utilizing a maximum number of their inductive components.

MODEL: 14-5 Communication 14 YRS: 1937-38 BANDS: 5, .55-60 mHz IF: 456 kHz FILTER: Crystal TUBES: 14, 6K7 rf, 6L7 mix, 6J7 hfo, 6K7 if, 6L7 if, 6R7 det/af1, 6C5 bfo, 6S7 noise amp, 6H6 noise rect, 6K7 avc amp, 6H6 avc rect, 2 25L6 af out, 5Z3 rect AF OUT: 12 W. REMARKS: Kit.

MODEL: DeJong "8" YRS: 1935-36 BANDS: 4, .54-25 mHz TUBES: 8 REMARKS: Kit.

MEISSNER

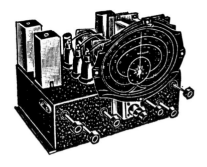

MODEL: All Wave "8" YRS: 1937-38 PRICE: $20.70 BANDS: 4, .54-43 mHz REMARKS: Kit with factory wired tuning assembly.

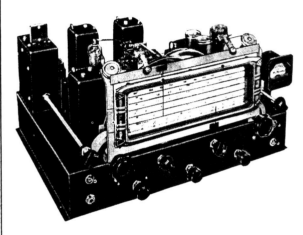

MODEL: Traffic Master YRS: 1938-43 PRICE: $81.90 less tubes and speaker BANDS: 5, .54-31 mHz IF: 456 kHz FILTER: Crystal TUBES: 14, 1853 rf, 6K8 mix, 6J7 hfo, 6L7 if1, 6K7 if2, 6H6 det/avc, 6H6 noise rect, 6J7 noise amp, 6SK7 (or 6SJ7) bfo, 6C8 phase inv, 2 6V6 p/p af out, VR150 vr, 5Y4 rect AF OUT: 8.5 W. REMARKS: Kit with preassembled, wired tuning unit.

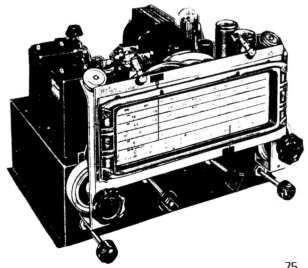

MEISSNER

MODEL Traffic Scout YRS: 1938-39 BANDS: 5, .54-31 mHz FILTER: None TUBES: 8, including one rf, one if. REMARKS: Kit with preassembled, wired tuning unit.

MODEL: Traffic Scout YRS: 1940 BANDS: 5, .54-32.4 mHz IF: 456 kHz FILTER: Crystal TUBES: 9, 1853 rf, 6K8 mix, 6J7 hfo, 2 6K7 if, 6Q7 det/avc/af1, 6SJ7 bfo, 6V6 af out, 5Y4 rect REMARKS: Kit with preassembled, wired tuning unit.

MILLEN

James Millen left National in 1939 to form his own company. The James Millen Manufacturing Co, Malden, Mass., produced high quality components and accessories. Millen designed two communications receivers for introduction after World War II. Plans were changed and they never made it to market.

MODEL: DPF-201 BANDS: .55-31.5 mHz TUBES: 6AK5 rf REMARKS: Weighs 80 lbs. Double conversion, sliding coil catacomb.

MODEL: DPF-501 BANDS: .55-41.5 mHz REMARKS: Weighs 107 lbs!

MONTGOMERY WARD

This large mail-order retailer has sold a number of communications receivers over the years.

MONTGOMERY WARD

MODEL: Professional Model 37 YRS: 1935 PRICE: $52.95 BANDS: 3, .54-18 mHz IF: 465 kHz FILTER: None TUBES: 7, 7B7 rf, 6A7 conv, 78 if, 75 det/avc/af1, 78 bfo, 42 af out, 80 rect REMARKS: Airplane dial, internal speaker. Built by Hallicrafters and appears identical to Hallicrafters Super-7.

MORROW

The Morrow Radio Manfucturing Co., 2794 Market St., Salem, Oregon, produced mobile communications equipment during the mid-1950's.

MODEL: MB-6 YRS: 1957-59 PRICE: $239.50 TYPE: Double conversion, tunable HFO BANDS: 5 Ham Bands, 10-80 mtrs TUBES: 13 REMARKS: Mobile type, separate power supply.

MORROW

MODEL: MBR-5 YRS: 1955-57 PRICE: $224.50
BANDS: 5, 10-80 mtrs TYPE: Double conversion, variable hfo IF: 1525, 200 kHz
FILTER: None TUBES: 13, 6BZ6 rf, 12AT7
mix1/hfo, 6BJ6 if1, 6BE6 mix2/xco, 6BJ6
if2, 6T8 det/bfo, 6AL5 noise rect, 12AT7
noise amp/meter amp, 6AL5 nl, 12AX7
af1/sq, 6C4 af2, 6AQ5 af out, 6BJ6 calib
REMARKS: Mobile type, separate power
supply.

MODEL: Falcon YRS: 1957 PRICE: $169
BANDS: 5, 75-10 mtrs TYPE: Dual conversion, tunable hfo REMARKS: Mobile type,
separate power supply. Available with
BC tuner installed as accessory.

MOSLEY

Mosley Electronics, 4610 North Lind-
bergh Blvd, Bridgeton, MO, manufactured
antennas. They attempted to enter the
amateur equipment market in 1961 with
an innovative ham band receiver.

MOSLEY

MODEL: CM-1 YRS: 1961-62 PRICE: $169.95
BANDS: 7 650 kHz bands, 80-10 mtrs TYPE:
Double conversion, fixed hfo. IF: 3500-
4100, 455 kHz FILTER: None TUBES: 5 + 2
semi diodes, 6AW8A mix1/xco, 6AW8A mix2/
vfo, 6AW8A if1/af1, 6AW8A if2/prod det,
6AW8A af out/bfo, 1N34 am det, 2F4 rect
AF OUT: 0.5 W.

MULTI-ELMAC

The Multi-Products Co., was located at
559 East Ten Mile Road, Hazel Park, Mich.,
during the early 1950's and at 21470 Cool-
idge Highway, Oak Park, Mich., after 1955.
They produced the Multi-Elmac line of
mobile equipment until 1962.

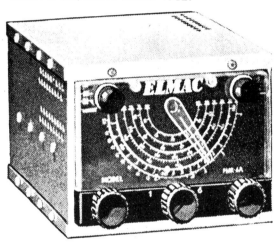

MODEL: PMR 6-A YRS: 1953-55 PRICE:
$134.50 BANDS: 6, BC + 10-80 mtrs TYPE:
Double conversion, variable hfo IF: 1600,
455 kHz FILTER: None TUBES: 10, 6BJ6 rf,
6BE6 mix, 6C4 hfo, 6BE6 conv, 2 6BJ6 if,
6AL5 det/nl, 12AT7 af1/bfo, 0B2 vr, 6BK5
af out AF OUT: 3.5 W. REMARKS: Mobile
type receiver, separate power supply.

MULTI-ELMAC

MODEL: PMR-7 YRS: 1955-57 PRICE: $159
BANDS: 7, BC + 160-10 mtrs TYPE: Double
conversion, variable hfo IF: 2238, 262 kHz
FILTER: 262 kHz L/C TUBES: 10, 6BZ6 rf,
6BE6 mix1, 6C4 hfo, 6BJ6 if, 6X8 mix2/xco,
6BA6 if, 6BJ7 det/anl/avc, 6AN8 af1/sq,
12AU7 bfo/amp, 6AQ5 af out REMARKS:
Mobile type receiver, external power
supply.

MODEL: PMR-7A YRS: 1958 PRICE: $159.50
REMARKS: Mobile type receiver, separate
power supply.

MODEL: PMR-8 YRS: 1960-62 PRICE: $189.50
BANDS: 7, BC + 80-6 mtrs TYPE: Double
conversion, variable hfo IF: 2238, 262 kHz
FILTER: 262 kHz L/C TUBES: 8 REMARKS:
Mobile type receiver, separate power
supply.

MODEL: PMR 12-A YRS: 1955 PRICE: $134.50
REMARKS: 12 volt version of the PMR 6-A.

NATIONAL

The National Company was established
in 1914 in Cambridge, MA. They manufactured mechanical parts, including toys,
until 1924 when they began producing the
famous Browning-Drake broadcast receiver
kit. In the same year they used their
mechanical expertise to begin producing
radio components including variable capacitors and the classic "velvet vernier"
dials.

James Millen joined National in 1928 as

NATIONAL

Chief Engineer and General Manager and
guided the company to the forefront of
the short wave receiver business where
they stayed until he left the company ten
years later. Millen was a mechanical engineer and the receivers designed during
his tenure reflected that background. He
was a ham and held the calls W2BYP,
W1AXL and W1HRX. Millen was also a prolific writer whose articles on the latest
developments at National appeared almost
monthly in the popular radio magazines of
the '20's and '30's.

Jim Millen's first receivers at National
were the "Thrill Box" series of regenerative sets produced during the late 1920's
and early 1930's. These included the famous SW-5 and SW-3.

Then, in July, 1932, National introduced the most advanced communications receiver of the time, the AGS.
This receiver was developed for Aircraft Ground Station use in conjunction
with the Airways Division of the U. S.
Dept. of Commerce. It was a nine tube
receiver with a tuned RF stage and
AVC. The set was advertised in QST for
affluent amateurs who could afford the
very best but few of them turned up
in ham shacks. There were not many affluent amateurs in 1932 and 1933.

Next came the FB-7, a stripped down
version of the AGS for ham station use,
in February, 1933. Selling for $26.46 the
little FB-7 came with one set of plug-in
coils but without a power supply. An
optional crystal filter was later offered
in a version designated the FBX.

Late in 1933 work began on a communications receiver which was destined to
become the most famous in history, a receiver which remained in production in re-
cognizable form for 30 years. The receiver was the HRO and was first mentioned
in print in Jim Millen's column in QST in
August, 1934. He said the set was designed for the ham bands and fell between
the FB-7 and AGS in price and performance. The first advertisement which appeared in the October, 1934, QST had a

NATIONAL

photo of a prototype which was quite different from the final version which started delivery in March, 1935.

Changes were apparently made late in the design of the HRO and it came on the market as a general coverage receiver and surpassed the AGS both in performance and price. The PW dial and gear drive, the ganged capacitors and the ganged coils and coil compartments are clasics of mechanical design.

Millen's mechanical engineering background was apparent again in the next receivers introduced by National in 1936, the general coverage NC-100 and the amateur band NC-101. These sets replaced the plug-in coils with a gear driven coil catacomb. The coils were contained in a die cast catacomb which was moved along a rail to bring the desired coil set into position. This scheme continued in use on the NC-200 and NC-2-40 series until 1949.

It is interesting that National did not employ the conventional coil switching method of band changing in any but their cheaper receivers until 1947. The HRO used the ganged plug-in coils to end in the early 1960's. Other receivers used the gear driven coil catacomb.

National's approach during the Millen years was to design and manufacture all the key components for their receivers including the tuning capacitors, IF transformers, coils and tuning mechanisms. The quality, electrically and mechanically, was superior and it is informative of National's philosophy that in 1937 when they introduced the medium priced NC-80 series they were apologetic in their advertising, saying, "Most amateurs do not need to be told that when a communications receiver is to be sold for as low a price as the NC-80 it is necessary to make compromises."

In 1939 National went public in spite of internal disagreement over the action. As a result, the following announ-

NATIONAL

cement appeared in June QST, "James Millen announces that on May first 1939, he completely withdrew from the National Company, Inc., in order to establish a new company. . .known as the James Millen Manufacturing Company, Inc." Thus began the decline of National. The company was never again a leading innovator in the commercial communications receiver business except for a brief time early in the solid state era.

During World War II National produced large quantities of equipment for the armed services, particularly the Navy. Prominent were many variations of the NC-100A and HRO receivers.

After the war National continued their prewar line of receivers essentially unchanged except for some cosmetic face lifts. In 1947 they introduced the NC-183, their first really new receiver since 1936. New for National, that is. The NC-183 was a rather conventional bandswitching receiver by the standards of other companies.

Like Hallicrafters, National tried to capitalize on their reputation in the short wave field by testing the consumer market with television receivers and high fidelity equipment. It turned out to be a competitive, money losing business and was soon abandoned.

During the 1950's and 1960's National was busy in military/defense electronics. Some of the prominent equipment during these decades were the WRR-2 super stable SSB receiver, standard receiver for Navy shipboard use, and the R-1490/GRR-17 high performance, solid-state communications receiver. Also noteworthy was the NC-2001 Atomichron, the first commercially available atomic primary time and frequency standard.

In 1955 National made a last attempt to regain its past glories in the amateur receiver field. They ran advertisements for several months hailing a new "dream receiver" which showed a cloth

NATIONAL

draped receiver with all its details hidden, like a statue prior to its unveiling. This turned out to be the NC-300 amateur band receiver. It was followed in 1958 by the improved NC-303. Unfortunately, like Hallicrafters, they misread the public's changing tastes. The advertisements boasted that the receiver was "massive in the modern manner." The modern manner turned out to be lighter, smaller high performance receivers which Collins (75S-1) and Drake (1-A) were about to introduce. The days of the heavy, massive receiver were dead.

National was a pioneer in the development of the solid-state receiver. The HRO-500, introduced in 1964, was the first completely solid-state receiver and was the first communications receiver to use a frequency synthesizer. Perhaps it was a little ahead of its time. The HRO-500 was popular and widely admired but it didn't save the company.

National Radio Company, the successor to National Company, exists today in Malden, MA, where it is in Chapter 11. It is a small, struggling company living on government contracts.

MODEL: AGL YRS: 1933-34 REMARKS: Long wave version of AGS with a Frequency Selector Switch substituted for the plug-in coils and Type "B" dial.

MODEL: AGS YRS: 1932 BANDS: 2.4-20 mHz IF: 500 kHz FILTER: None TUBES: 9, 4 236, 4 237, 238 REMARKS: Plug-in coils, separ-

NATIONAL

ate power supply, round Type "N" dial. Developed for Aircraft Ground Stations in conjunction with Airways Division of the U. S. Dept. of Commerce.

MODEL: AGS (Variation 1) YRS: 1933 PRICE: $161.70 BANDS: 5, 1.5-20 mHz IF: 500 kHz FILTER: None TUBES: 9, 236 rf, 236 mix, 236 hfo, 2 236 if, 237 det, 236 avc, 237 bfo, 238 af out REMARKS: Plug-in coils, separate power supply. Bandspread coils available.

MODEL: AGS (Variation 2) YRS: 1933 BANDS: 5, 1.5-20 mHz IF: 500 kHz FILTER: None TUBES: 9, 236 rf, 236 mix, 236 hfo, 2 236 if, 237 det, 236 avc, 237 bfo, 89 af out REMARKS: Plug-in coils, separate power supply. Change from Variation 1: audio output tube changed to 89.

MODEL: AGS (Variation 3) YRS: 1933-34 BANDS: 5, 1.5-20 mHz IF: 500 kHz FILTER: None TUBES: 9, 236 rf, 236 mix, 236 hfo, 2 236 if, 237 det, 236 bfo, 236 avc, 89 af out REMARKS: Plug-in coils, separate power supply. Changes from Variation 2: BFO tube changed to 236.

MODEL: AGS (Variation 4) YRS: 1934 PRICE: $265 (list) BANDS: 5, 1.5-20 mHz IF: 500 kHz FILTER: None TUBES: 9, 3 236, 237, 89, 77, 3 78 REMARKS: Plug-in coils, separate power supply. Changes from Variation 3: added a 77 and 3 78's, replacing 4 236's.

MODEL: AGS (Variation 5) YRS: 1933 REMARKS: The standard round dial replaced with a velvet vernier Type "B" (SW-3).

MODEL: AGS-X YRS: 1933-34 PRICE: $295 (list) FILTER: Crystal REMARKS: AGS with crystal filter. Adds CW OSC tuning control in upper left and crystal selectivity and ser/par controls in upper right.

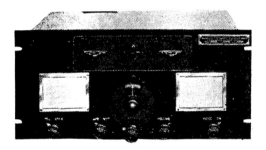

MODEL: AGU YRS: 1933 REMARKS: AGS with ganged plug-in coils and Type "B" dial.

MODEL: FB-7 YRS: 1933-34 PRICE: $26.46 BANDS: 6, 1.5-33 mHz IF: 500 kHz FILTER: None TUBES: 7, (2.5 V. version) 57 mix,

24 hfo, 2 58 if, 56 det, 59 af out, 24 bfo (6.3 V. version) 77 mix, 36 hfo, 2 78 if, 37 det, 89 af out, 36 bfo REMARKS: External power supply, plug-in coils. Originally offered only to 20 mHz with five sets of coils.

MODEL: FB7-A YRS: 1933-34 PRICE: $31.16 REMARKS: FB-7 with air tuned (vs compression mica) IF transformers.

MODEL: FBX YRS: 1933-34 PRICE: $38.22 FILTER: Crystal REMARKS: FB-7 with crystal filter.

MODEL: FBX-A YRS: 1933-34 PRICE: $42.93 FILTER: Crystal REMARKS: FBX with air tuned (vs mica compression) IF transformers.

NATIONAL

MODEL: HRO (Prototype) YRS: 1934 PRICE: $167.70 Bands: 6. 0.5-30 mHz IF: 456 kHz FILTER: Crystal TUBES: 9, (2.5 V. model) 2 58 rf, 57 mix, 57 hfo, 2 58 if, 2B7 det/avc/af1, 2A5 af out, 57 bfo, (6.3 V. model) 2 6D6 rf, 6C6 mix, 6C6 hfo, 2 6D6 if, 6B7 det/avc/af1, 42 af out, 6C6 bfo AF OUT: 1.5 W. REMARKS: Plug-in coils, separate power supply. This model shown in advertisements from Oct., 1934, thru Jan., 1935, had no RF Gain, BFO Pitch controls or "S" meter switch. Round, un-skirted knobs. Probably never shipped this model.

MODEL: HRO (Variation 1) YRS: 1934-35 REMARKS: Details same as HRO (Proto-type) except added RF Gain, BFO Pitch and "S" meter switch, replaced round knobs with bar knobs with round skirts. no markings on B+ and AVC switches and selectivity control except for rack mount version (pictured) which has engraved markings. White push type "S" meter switch.

Courtesy AWA and AWA Review

NATIONAL

MODEL: HRO (Variation 2) YRS: 1935-36 REMARKS: Added panel light to left of selectivity switch, calibration charts changed to white on black, "S" meter switch changed to push/pull type.

MODEL: HRO (Variation 3) YRS: 1936-38 REMARKS: Added engraved panel markings for B+, AVC and selectivity. Photos still show round IF transformers and black chassis.

MODEL: HRO (Variation 4) YRS: 1938-1943 REMARKS: Black bakelite dial, rectang-ular IF cans, otherwise same.

MODEL: HRO (Variation 5) YRS: 1943-45
REMARKS: This variation used for HRO-5,
-M, -W, et al. AVC and B+ switches have
circumferential metal labels, selectivity
control changed to bar knob with cir-
cular skirt, "S" meter switch changed to
toggle, crystal mounted inside filter
case.

MODEL: HRO-C REMARKS: HRO in table
rack with SPC coil storage unit, power
supply and speaker.

MODEL: HRO (Variation 6) YRS: 1946-47
REMARKS: Rectangular bakelite "S"
meter, noise limiter control added between PW dial and phone jack, printed
metal charts on coil gangs. Used for
HRO-5A1, last receiver using the original HRO basic look.

MODEL: HRO-B TUBES: 9, 2 6D6 rf, 6C6
mix, 6C6 hfo, 2 6D6 if, 6B7 det/avc/af1,
42 af out, 6C6 bfo AF OUT: 1.5 W. RE-
MARKS: Variation 4, battery model op-
timized to operate with 180 V. B+ at 55
mA (vs 230 V./75 mA.)

MODEL: HRO-B-JR REMARKS: Ref. HRO-B
and HRO-JR.

MODEL: HRO-JR YRS: 1936-43 PRICE: $99.00
REMARKS: HRO less crystal filter, "S"
meter and bandspread.

MODEL: HRO-M YRS: 1944-45 BANDS: 9, .05-30 mHz IF: 456 kHz FILTER: Crystal TUBES: 9, 2 6D6 rf, 6C6 mix, 6C6 hfo, 2 6D6 if, 6B7 det/avc/af1, 42 af out, 6C6 bfo AF OUT: 1.5 W. REMARKS: Variation 5, no bandspread.

MODEL: HRO-M-RR REMARKS: Same tubes as HRO-M. Difference not known.

MODEL: HRO-M-TM REMARKS: Tubes same as HRO-M. Difference not known.

MODEL: HRO-MX REMARKS: Tubes same as HRO-M. Difference not known.

MODEL: HRO-S YRS: 1934 TUBES: 10, same as HRO (Prototype), 2.5 V. series, with addition of 80 rect. REMARKS: Built-in power supply. Doubt if any of these were ever sold.

MODEL: HRO-SPC REMARKS: HRO in 24½" table rack including HRO, power supply, speaker and 5 compartment coil storage rack. See HRO-C.

MODEL: HRO-SR REMARKS: HRO-SR (senior) designation sometimes used for standard HRO after introduction of the HRO-JR.

MODEL: HRO-W YRS:1944-45 BANDS: 9, .05-30 mHz IF: 456 kHz FILTER: Crystal TUBES: 9, 2 6K7 rf, 6J7 mix, 6J7 hfo, 2 6K7 if, 6SQ7 det/avc/af1, 6V6 af out, 6J7 bfo AF OUT: 1.5 W. REMARKS: Variation 5, similar to HRO-5. No bandspread, tropicalized, built for Signal Corps.

MODEL: HRO-5 YRS: 1944-45 BANDS: 9, .05-30 mHz IF: 456 kHz FILTER: Crystal TUBES: 9, same as HRO-W REMARKS: Separate P/S, plug-in coils, no bandspread, built to JAN specs.

MODEL: HRO-5R REMARKS: Rack mounted.

MODEL: HRO-5T REMARKS: Table model.

MODEL: HRO-5A YRS: 1945-46 REMARKS:

Same as HRO-5 except civilian construction, has bandspread.

MODEL: HRO-5RA REMARKS: HRO-5A table model.

MODEL: HRO-5TA REMARKS: HRO-5A rack model.

MODEL: HRO-5TAL REMARKS: No information.

MODEL: HRO-5C REMARKS: Deluxe installation containing an HRO-5A1 and an SPC unit (Power supply, coil container and speaker.)

MODEL: HRO-5A1 YRS: 1946-47 PRICE: $274.35 BANDS: 9, .05-30 mHz IF: 456 kHz FILTER: Crystal TUBES: 11, 2 6K7 rf, 6J7 mix, 6J7 hfo, 2 6K7 if, 6SQ7 det/avc/af1, 6V6 af out, 6J7 bfo, 6J5 nl amp, 6H6 nl rect AF OUT: 1.5 W. REMARKS: Plug-in coils, separate power supply. Adds noise limiter control to front panel. See Variation 6.

MODEL: HRO-5TA-1 REMARKS: HRO-5A1 in cabinet for table use.

MODEL: HRO-5RA-1 REMARKS: HRO-5A1 for rack mounting.

MODEL: HRO-6 REMARKS: No information.

MODEL: HRO-7 YRS: 1947-49 PRICE: $311.36 BANDS: 9, .05-30 mHz IF: 456 kHz FILTER: Crystal TUBES: 12, 2 6K7 rf, 6J7 mix, 6C4 hfo, 6J7/6K7 if1, 6K7 if2, 6H6

NATIONAL

det/avc, 6J7 bfo, 6H6 nl, 6SJ7 af1, 6V6 af out, 0A2 vr AF OUT: 1.5 W. REMARKS: Plug-in coils, separate power supply. New, streamlined cabinet.

MODEL: HRO-7R REMARKS: Rack mount version.

MODEL: HRO-7T REMARKS: Table model.

MODEL: HRO-7C YRS: 1948-49 PRICE: $358 REMARKS: HRO-7 in 29" cabinet rack with coil storage compartments, speaker and power supply.

MODEL: HRO-12S REMARKS: No information.

MODEL: HRO-50 YRS: 1950 PRICE: $349 BANDS: 9, .05-30 mHz IF: 455 kHz FILTER: Crystal TUBES: 15, 2 6BA6 rf, 6BE6 mix, 6C4 hfo, 2 6K7 if, 6H6 det/avc, 6H6 anl, 6SJ7 af1, 6SN7 phase split/mtr amp, 6J7 bfo, 6 6V6 p/p af out, 5V4 rect, 0B2 vr AF OUT: 8 W. REMARKS: Plug-in coils. PW and direct reading, slide rule dial.

NATIONAL

MODEL: HRO-50-1 YRS: 1951-52 PRICE: $383.50 BANDS: 9, .05-30 mHz IF: 455 kHz FILTER: Crystal plus 12 455 kHz L/C circuits TUBES: 16, 2 6BA6 rf, 6BE6 mix, 6C4 hfo, 6K7 if1, 2 6SG7 if2/3, 6H6 det/avc, 6H6 nl, 6SN7 phase inv/mtr amp, 6SJ7 af1, 2 6V6 p/p af out, 6J7 bfo, 0B2 vr, 5V4 rect AF OUT: 8 W. REMARKS: Plug-in coils. HRO-50 with added IF stage and cascaded IF transformers.

MODEL: HRO-50R1 REMARKS: Rack mount.

MODEL: HRO-50T1 REMARKS: Table model.

MODEL: HRO-60 YRS: 1952-64 PRICE: $483.50 (1952), $745 (1961) BANDS: 10, .05-54 mHz TYPE: Double Conversion IF: 2010, 456 kHz FILTER: Crystal plus 12 455 kHc L/C circuits TUBES: 18, 2 6BA6 rf, 6BE6 mix, 6C4 hfo, 6BE6 conv2, 3 6SG7 if, 6H6 det/avc, 6H6 nl, 6SN7 phase inv/mtr amp, 6SJ7 af1, 2 6V6 p/p af out, 6SJ7 bfo, 0B2 vr, 4H4C current reg, 5V4 rect AF OUT: 8 W. REMARKS: Plug-in coils.

MODEL: NC-33 YRS: 1948-50 PRICE: $57.50 BANDS: 4, 0.5-35 mHz IF: 456 kHz FILTER: None TUBES: 6, 12SA7 conv, 12SG7 if, 12H6 det/avc/nl, 12SL7 af1/bfo 35L6 af out, 35Z5 rect REMARKS: AC/DC, internal speaker.

MODEL: NC-44 YRS: 1938-40 PRICE: $49.50 IF: 456 kHz FILTER: None TUBES: 7, 6K8 conv, 2 6L7 if, 6K7 det/avc, 6J7 bfo, 25L6 af out, 25Z5 rect REMARKS: AC/DC.

MODEL: NC-44A REMARKS: Transformer operated, AC only version of NC-44.

MODEL: NC-44B REMARKS: 6 V. battery operated version of NC-44.

MODEL: NC-45 YRS: 1941-45 PRICE: $49.50 BANDS: 4, .55-30 mHz FILTER: None TUBES: 8, 6K8 conv, 2 6L7 if, 6SQ7 det/avc/af1, 6H6 nl, 6J7 bfo, 25L6 af out, 25Z5 rect REMARKS: AC/DC, NC-44 with added NL and new detector tube.

MODEL: NC-45A REMARKS: AC version of NC-45 with transformer operated power supply.

MODEL: NC-45B REMARKS: 6 V. battery operated version of NC-45.

MODEL: NC-46 Prototype REMARKS: The receiver pictured above appeared in the 1946 ARRL Handbook. Later ads showed the receiver below.

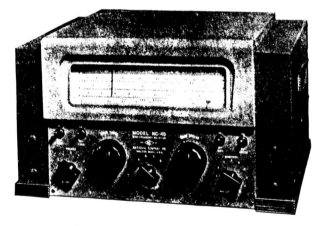

MODEL: NC-46 YRS: 1945-47 PRICE: $107.40 BANDS: 4, .55-30 mHz IF: 455 kHz FILTER: None TUBES: 10, 6K8 conv, 2 6SG7 if, 6H6 det/nl, 6SF7 avc amp/rect, 6SJ7 bfo, 6SC7 af1/af inv, 2 25L6 p/p af out, 25Z5 rect AF OUT: 3 W. REMARKS: AC/DC.

NATIONAL

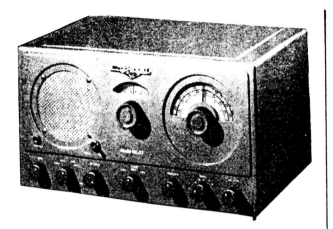

MODEL: NC-57 YRS: 1947-51 PRICE: $89.50 BANDS: 5, .54-55 mHz IF: 455 kHz FILTER: None TUBES: 9, 6SG7 rf, 6SB7Y conv, 2 6SG7 if, 6H6 det/avc/nl, 6SL7 af1/bfo, 6V6 af out, 0D3 vr, 5Y3 rect REMARKS: Internal speaker.

MODEL: NC-57B YRS: 1951 PRICE: $99.50 BANDS: 5, .55-55 mHz IF: 455 kHz FILTER: None TUBES: 9, 6SG7 rf, 6SB7Y conv, 2 6H6 if, 6H6 det/avc/nl, 6SL7 af1/bfo, 6V6 af out, VR150 vr, 5Y3 rect REMARKS: Differences not known.

MODEL: NC-57C BANDS: 5, .19-.41, .54-34 mHz REMARKS: Same as NC-57B except frequency coverage.

MODEL: NC-57M YRS: 1951 BANDS: 5, .19-.41, 54-34 mHz IF: 455 kHz FILTER: None TUBES: 9, 6SG7 rf, 6SB7Y conv, 2 6SG7 if, 6H6 det/avc/anl, 6SL7 af1/bfo, 25L6 af out, 0A3/VR75 vr, 25Z6 rect REMARKS: AC/DC version on NC-57C intended for marine use.

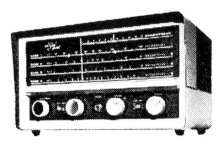

MODEL: NC-60 YRS: 1958-61 PRICE: $59.95 BANDS: 4, .54-31 mHz IF: 455 kHz FILTER: None TUBES: 5, 12BE6 conv, 12BA6 if/

NATIONAL

bfo, 12AV6 det/avc/af1, 50C5 af out, 35W4 rect REMARKS: Internal speaker, AC/DC. Restyled, redesigned SW-54.

MODEL: NC-66 YRS: 1957-61 PRICE: $129.95 BANDS: 5, .15-.4, .5-23 mHz FILTER: None TUBES: 5 + sel rect, 1U4 rf, 1L6 conv, 1U4 if/bfo, 1U5 det/avc/nl, 3V4 af out, sel rect REMARKS: AC/DC/ battery, internal speaker.

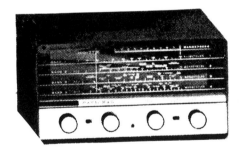

MODEL: NC-77X YRS: 1964 BANDS: 4 REMARKS: No other information.

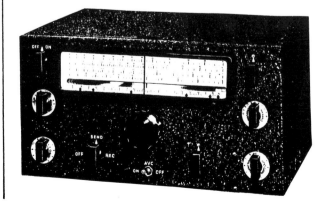

NATIONAL

MODEL: NC-80X YRS: 1937-38 PRICE: $88.00
BANDS: 4, .55-30 mHz IF: 1560 kHz FILTER:
crystal TUBES: 10, 6L7 mix, 6J7 hfo, 3 6K7
if, 6C5 det, 6B8 avc, 6J7 bfo, 25L6 af out
25Z5 rect AF OUT: 2 W. REMARKS: AC/DC,
direct reading dial, movable coil rack.

MODEL: NC-81X YRS: 1937-39 PRICE: $88.00
BANDS: 5, 160, 80, 40, 20, 10 mtr ham
bands REMARKS: Ham band model of
NC-80X.

MODEL: NC-88 World Master YRS: 1953-56
PRICE: $119.95 BANDS: 4, .54-40 mHz IF:
455 kHZ FILTER: None TUBES: 9, 6BA6 rf,
6BE6 mix, 6C4 hfo, 2 6BD6 if, 6AL5 det/
avc/nl, 12AX7 af1/bfo, 6AQ5 af out, 5Y3
rect AF OUT: 1.5W. REMARKS: Internal
speaker. NC-98 without crystal and "S"
meter, successor to NC-57.

MODEL: NC-98 YRS: 1954-56 PRICE: $149.95
BANDS: 4, .55-40 mHz IF: 455 kHz FILTER:
Crystal TUBES: 9, 6BA6 rf, 6BE6 mix, 6C4
hfo, 2 6BD6 if, 6AL5 det/avc/nl, 12AX7

NATIONAL

af1/bfo/mtr amp, 6AQ5 af out, 5Y3 rect
AF OUT: 1.5 W.

MODEL: NC-98SW REMARKS: NC-98 with
bandspread scales calibrated for SW BC
bands.

MODEL: NC-100 YRS: 1936-38 PRICE: $105
BANDS: 5, .54-30 mHz IF: 455 kHz FILTER:
None TUBES: 12, 6K7 rf, 6J7 mix, 6K7 hfo,
2 6K7 if, 6C5 det, 6J7 bfo, 6J7 avc, 6E5
tun eye, 2 6F6 p/p af out, 80 rect AF
OUT: 10 W. REMARKS: PW dial, movable
coil rack, tuning eye.

MODEL: NC-100 (Battery) TUBES: 10, 6K7
rf, 6J7 mix, 2 6K7 if, 6C5 det, 6J7 bfo,
6J7 avc, 6E6 tun eye, 6F6 af out AF OUT:
2 W. REMARKS: Battery model, operates
on B+ of 180 V. at 35 mA.

MODEL: NC-100A YRS: 1938-45 PRICE:
$120 BANDS: 5, .54-30 mHz IF: 455 kHz
FILTER: None TUBES: 11 REMARKS: New
cabinet, "S" meter in place of eye,
direct reading dial in place of PW.

MODEL: NC-100A (Special) BANDS: 5, 0.2-
0.4, 1.3-30 mHz REMARKS: NC-100A with
low frequency band.

MODEL: NC-100ASC REMARKS: No info.

MODEL: NC-100ASD BANDS: 5, 0.2-0.4,
1.3-30 mHz IF: 456 kHz FILTER: None
TUBES: 10, 6K7 rf, 6J7 mix, 6J7 hfo,
2 6K7 if, 6C8 det/nl, 6F8 af1/avc, 6J7

NATIONAL

bfo, 6V6 af out, 5Z3 rect AF OUT: 2 W.
REMARKS: Built to Signal Corps stand-
ards. Available for either 115 V., 50/60
Hz or 115 V., 25 Hz.

MODEL: NC-100S REMARKS: Special NC-100
with 12" speaker (vs 10").

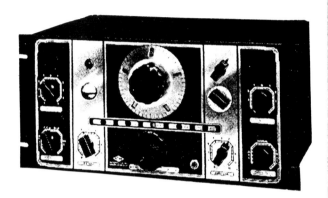

MODEL: NC-100X PRICE: $127.50 FILTER:
Crystal REMARKS: NC-100 with crystal
filter.

MODEL: NC-100X (Battery) FILTER:
Crystal REMARKS: NC-100 (Battery)
with crystal filter.

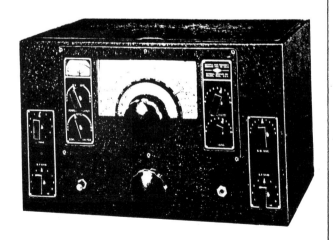

MODEL: NC-100XA PRICE: $142.50 FILTER:
Crystal REMARKS: NC-100A with crystal
filter.

NATIONAL

MODEL: NC-100XA (Variation) REMARKS:
Note additional control and different
placement of controls.

MODEL: NC-100XA (Special) BANDS: 5,
0.2-0.4, 1.3-30 mHz REMARKS: NC-100XA
with low frequency band.

MODEL: NC-100XS REMARKS: Special
NC-100X with 12" speaker (vs 10")

MODEL: NC-100XAM REMARKS: No information available.

MODEL: NC101X YRS: 1936-39 PRICE:
$125 BANDS: 5, 160, 80, 40, 20, 10 mtr ham
bands IF: 455 kHz FILTER: Crystal TUBES:
12, 6K7 rf, 6J7 mix, 6K7 hfo, 2 6K7 if, 6C5
det, 6J7 avc, 6J7 bfo, 2 6F6 p/p af out,
6E5 tun eye, 80 rect AF OUT: 10 W.
REMARKS: Ham band only version of
NC-100. PW dial, movable coil catacomb,
tuning eye.

MODEL: NC-101X (Variation) REMARKS: "S" meter replaces tuning eye, adds push-pull "S" meter switch.

MODEL: NC-101X (Battery) TUBES: 10, 6K7 rf, 6J7 mix, 6K7 hfo, 2 6K7 if, 6C5 det, 6J7 avc, 6J7 bfo, 6F6 af out, 6E5 tun eye AF OUT: 2 W. REMARKS: Battery version of NC-101X. Operates from B+ of 180 V. at 35 mA.

MODEL: NC-101XA YRS: 1939-41 PRICE: $129 BANDS: 5, 160, 80, 40, 20, 10 mtr ham bands IF: 455 kHz FILTER: Crystal TUBES: 11 REMARKS: Ham band only version of NC-100A New direct reading dial, noise limiter, "S" meter. Retains movable coil catacomb.

MODEL: NC-105 YRS: 1962-63 PRICE: $119.95 BANDS: 4, .55-30 mHz IF: 455 kHz FILTER: Regenerative if TUBES: 6, 6BE6 conv, 2 6BA6 if, 6T8 det/anl/af1, 6AW8 det/bfo/af out, 6X4 rect REMARKS: Internal speaker.

MODEL: NC-109 YRS: 1957-60 PRICE: $199.95 BANDS: 4, .54-40 mHz IF: 455 kHz FILTER: Crystal TUBES: 11, 6BA6 rf, 6BE6 mix, 6C4 hfo, 2 6BA6 if, 6AL5 det/avc/nl, 6BE6 prod det, 12AT7 af1/bfo/meter amp, 6AQ5 af out, 0B2 vr, 5Y3 rect AF OUT: 1.5 W.

MODEL: NC-120 REMARKS: Similar to RAO. No other information available.

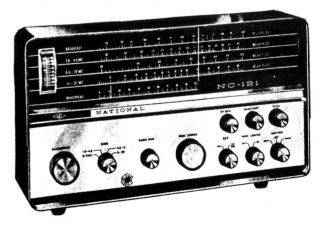

MODEL: NC-121 YRS: 1963-66 PRICE: $129.95 BANDS: 4, .54-30 mHz FILTER: Q multiplier REMARKS: Internal speaker.

MODEL: NC-125 YRS: 1950-55 PRICE: $149-50 BANDS: 4, .55-36 mHz FILTER: None TUBES: 11, 6SG7 rf, 6SB7Y conv, 2 6SG7 if 6H6 det/avc/anl, 6SL7 af1/bfo, 6V6 af out, 6SL7 phase shift, 6SL7 boost-rej REMARKS: Built-in Select-O-Ject.

MODEL: NC-127 REMARKS: No information available.

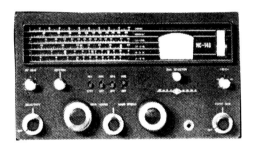

MODEL: NC-140 YRS: 1963-64 PRICE: $189.95 TYPE: Double conversion FILTER: Q multiplier REMARKS: Dual bandspread dials for ham and SWL.

MODEL: NC-155 YRS: 1961-63 PRICE: $199.95 BANDS: 6, 80, 40, 20, 10, 6 mtr ham bands TYPE: Double conversion IF: 2215, 230 kHz FILTER: 230 kHz L/C TUBES: 10, 6BZ6 rf, 6BE6 conv1, 6BE6 conv2, 2 6BA6 if, 6T8 det/agc/nl/af1, 12AX7 prod det/bfo, 6CW5 af out, 0B2 vr, 5Y3 rect AF OUT: 1 W. REMARKS: Ham band version of the NC-190.

MODEL: NC-156 BANDS: 0.3-1.2, 1.7-16 mHz REMARKS: Navy version of NC-100A with two RF stages. Ref: RBH.

MODEL: NC-173 YRS: 1947-1951 PRICE: $189.50 IF: 455 kHz FILTER: Crystal TUBES: 13, 6SG7 rf, 6SA7 mix, 6J5 hfo, 2 6SG7 if, 6H6 det/avc, 6H6 nl, 6SJ7 af1, 6AC7 avc amp, 6SJ7 bfo, 6V6 af out, 0D3 vr, 5Y3 rect AF OUT: 3.5 W.

MODEL: NC-173R REMARKS: Rack model.

MODEL: NC-173T REMARKS: Table model.

NATIONAL

NATIONAL

MODEL: NC-183 YRS: 1947-52 PRICE: $269
BANDS: 5, .54-31 mHz IF: 455 kHz FILTER:
Crystal TUBES: 16, 2 6SG7 rf, 6SA7 mix,
6J5 hfo, 2 6SG7 if, 6H6 det/avc, 6SJ7 bfo,
6AC7 avc amp, 6H6 nl, 6SJ7 af1, 6J5 phase
inv, 2 6V6 p/p af out, VR-150 vr, 5U4 rect
AF OUT: 8 W.

MODEL: NC-183R REMARKS: Rack model.

MODEL: NC-183T REMARKS: Table model.

MODEL: NC-183D YRS: 1952-58 PRICE:
$369.50 BANDS: 5, .54-55 mHz TYPE: Double
conversion IF: 1720, 455 kHz FILTER:
Crystal TUBES: 17, 2 6BA6 rf, 6BE6 conv1,
6BE6 conv2, 3 6BA6 if, 6AL5 det/avc,
6AH6 avc amp, 6SJ7 bfo, 6AL5 nl, 6SJ7 af1,
6SN7 phase inv/mtr amp, 2 6V6 p/p af out,
0B2 vr, 5U4 rect AF OUT: 8 W. REMARKS:
Dual conversion, new crystal filter, new
noise limiter, better sensitivity.

MODEL: NC-188 YRS: 1957-59 PRICE:
$159.95 BANDS: 4, .54-40 mHz FILTER: None
TUBES: 9, 6BA6 rf, 6BE6 mix, 6C4 hfo,
2 6BA6 if, 6AL5 det/avc/anl, 12AT7 af1/
bfo, 6AQ5 af out, 5Y3 rect AF OUT: 1.5 W.

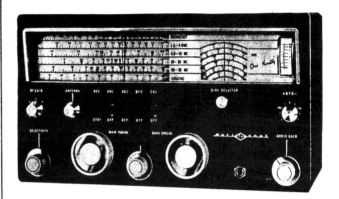

MODEL: NC-190 YRS: 1961-64 PRICE: $199.50
BANDS: 5, .54-30 mHz TYPE: Double conversion, tunable HFO IF: 2215, 230 kHz
FILTER: 230 kHz L/C TUBES: 10, 6BZ6 rf,
6BE6 conv1, 6BE6 conv2, 2 6BA6 if, 6T8
det/agc/nl/af1, 12AX7 prod det/bfo, 6CW5
af out, 0B2 vr, 5Y3 rect AF OUT: 1 W.
REMARKS: Selectable SWL or ham bandspread.

MODEL: NC-200 YRS: 1940-43 PRICE: $147.50
BANDS: 10, 6 general coverage bands .49-
30 mHz, 4 ham bands 10, 20, 40, 80 mtrs
FILTER: Crystal TUBES: 12 AF OUT: 8 W.
RJEMARKS: Ten range calibrated dial,
movable coil catacomb.

NATIONAL

NATIONAL

MODEL: NC-200RG REMARKS: Rack Model.

MODEL: NC-200TG REMARKS: Table model.

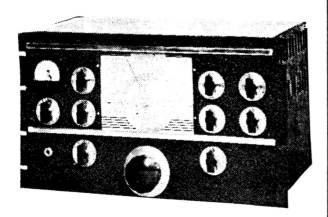

MODEL: NC-2-40 YRS: 1943-44 PRICE:
$169.50 BANDS: 6, .49-30 mHz IF: 455 kHz
FILTER: Crystal TUBES: 13, 6SK7 rf, 6K8
mix, 6J5 hfo, 6K7 if1, 6SK7 if2, 6C8 det/
nl, 6SJ7 bfo, 6SJ7 avc amp, 6J5 af1,
6F8 phase inv, 2 6V6 p/p af out, 80 rect
AF OUT: 6 W. REMARKS: Successor to
NC-200, movable coil catacombs.

MODEL: NC-2-40D YRS: 1946-49 PRICE:
$225 BANDS: 10 bands, 80, 40, 20, 10
mtr ham bands, 6 general coverage .49-
30 mHz IF: 455 kHz FILTER: Crystal
TUBES: 12, 6SK7 rf, 6K8 mix, 6J5 hfo,
6K7 if1, 6SK7 if2, 6SL7 det/nl, 6V6 avc,
6SJ7 bfo, 6SN7 phase inv, 2 6V6 p/p
af out, 5Y3 rect AF OUT: 8 W. REMARKS:
Movable coil catacombs.

MODEL: NC-2-40DR REMARKS: Rack Model.

MODEL: NC-2-40DT REMARKS: Table Model

MODEL: NC-2-40S PRICE: $189.50 BANDS:
6, 0.2-18 mHz REMARKS: Same as NC-2-40
except frequency coverage.

MODEL: NC-2-40C YRS: 1945-46 PRICE:
$225 BANDS: 6, .49-30 mHz IF: 455 kHz
FILTER: Crystal TUBES: 12 AF OUT: 8 W.

MODEL: NC-2-40CS BANDS: 6, 0.2-0.4,
1-30 mHz REMARKS: Same as NC-2-40C
except frequency coverage.

MODEL: NC-270 YRS: 1960-64 PRICE: $249.95
BANDS: 6, 80, 40, 20, 10(2), 6 mtrs TYPE:
Double conversion, tunable HFO IF: 2215,
230 kHz FILTER: 230 kHz L/C "ferrite fil-

ter" TUBES: 10, 6BZ6 rf, 6BE6 conv1, 6BE6 conv2, 2 6BA6 if, 6BA6 prod det, 12AU7 calib/bfo, 6T8 det/avc/anl/af1, 6CW5 af out, 0B2 vr, 5Y3 rect AF OUT: 3 W. REMARKS: Cabinet color, "Cosmic Blue."

MODEL: NC-300 YRS: 1955-58 PRICE: $349.95 BANDS: 7, 10-160 mtr ham bands plus 3 positions, 5 mHz wide, for 1¼, 2 and 6 mtr converters. TYPE: Double conversion IF: 2215, 80 kHz FILTER: 2215 crystal and 80 kHz L/C TUBES: 13, 6BZ6 rf, 6BA7 mix, 6AH6 hfo, 6BE6 conv2, 2 6BJ6 if, 6AL5 det/anl, 6BE6 prod det/ bfo, 12AT7 af1/mtr amp, 6AQ5 af out, 4H4-C curr reg, 0B2 vr, 5Y3 rect AF OUT: 1 W. REMARKS: Optional 1¼, 2, 6 meter converters. Ad says, "Massive in the modern manner."

MODEL: NC-303 YRS: 1958-62 PRICE: $449.95 BANDS: 7, 10-160 mtr ham bands plus 3 positions, 5 mHz wide, for 1¼, 2 and 6 mtr converters. TYPE: Double conversion IF: 2215, 80 kHz FILTER: 80 kHz L/C, Q multiplier TUBES: 15, 6BZ6 rf, 6BA7 mix 6AH6 hfo, 6BE6 mix2/xco, 2 6BJ6

if, 6AL5 det/anl, 6BE6 prod det/bfo, 6AL5 ssb-cw nl, 12AT7 af1/mtr amp, 12AX7 Q mult, 6AQ5 af out, 4H4-C curr reg, 0B2 vr, 5Y3 rect AF OUT: 1 W. REMARKS: Changes from NC-300: eliminated 2215 kHz crystal filter, added 80 kHz Q multiplier, new SSB/CW noise limiter, improved AVC.

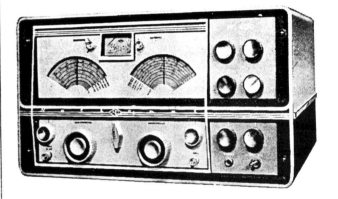

MODEL: NC-400 YRS: 1959-64 PRICE: $895 BANDS: 7, .54-31 mHz TYPE: Double conversion, tunable HFO IF: 1720, 455 kHz FILTER: Crystal, optional mechanical filters TUBES: 18, 2 6BZ6 rf, 2 6BE6 mix1, 6BZ7 hfo/fix chan xco, 6BE6 mix2/xco, 3 6BA6 if, 6AL5 det/avc/anl, 6BE6 prod det, 6U8 bfo, 6AL5 mnl, 12AT7 af1/mtr amp, 6AQ5 af out, 4H4-C curr reg, 0B2 vr, 5Y3 rect AF OUT: 1 W. REMARKS: Provision for five crystal controlled channels.

MODEL: SW-54 YRS: 1951-58 PRICE: $49.95 ($59.95 '56) BANDS: 4, .54-30 mHz IF: 455 kHz FILTER: None TUBES: 5, 12BE6 conv, 12BA6 if/bfo, 12AV6 det/avc/af1, 50C5 af out, 35Z5 rect AF OUT: 1.8W. REMARKS: AC/DC, internal speaker.

MODEL: NRCL YRS: 1944-45 REMARKS: Part of NCRM dual diversity system. PW dial, movable coil catacombs.

MODEL: BC-903-A YRS: WW II BANDS: 0.54-30 mHz FILTER: None REMARKS: Navy version of NC-100A.

MODEL: FRR-59A BANDS: 4, 2-32 mHz TYPE: Triple conversion, fixed HFO IF: 1625-1725, 220, 80 kHz TUBES: 64 plus 24 semi diodes (See WRR-2) REMARKS: AM/SSB/CW, digital readout, similar to WRR-2, q.v., but not mechanically interchangeable.

MODEL: AN/GRR-3 YRS: WW-II REMARKS: NC-100ASC

MODEL: R-115 YRS: WW-II 6, 0.2-0.4, .49-18 mHz FILTER: None TUBES: 13, 4 117N7, 3 12SK7, 12K8, 12J5, 12SC7, 12C8, 12SR7, 12SJ7 REMARKS: AC/DC, similar to NC-200 but less bandspread and crystal filter. Made for US Coast Guard.

MODEL: R-140 REMARKS: HRO-5

MODEL: R-211 REMARKS: HRO

Courtesy Antique Radio Classified and Henry Rogers.

MODEL: RAO-1 thru -8 YRS: WW-II BANDS: 5, .54-30 mHz FILTER: Crystal IF: 455 kHz TUBES: 11, 2 6K7 rf, 6J7 mix, 6J5 hfo, 2 6K7 if, 6C8 det/nl, 6J7 bfo, 6F8 af1/avc, 6V6 af out, 5Z3 rect REMARKS: Built for US Navy, similar to NC100XA with added RF stage bolted/welded to rear of cabinet with separate variable capacitor and coil catacomb ganged to main receiver controls. Ref: NC-120. Photo is of receiver built by Wells-Gardner.

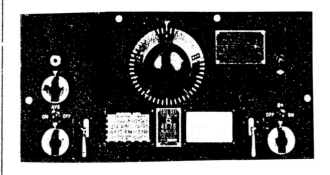

MODEL: RAS-1 thru -5 YRS: 1940-44 BANDS: 7, .19-30 mHz FILTER: None IF: 175 kHz TUBES: 9, 2 6D6 rf, 6C6 mix, 6C6 hfo, 2 6D6 if, 6F8 det/avc, 6C6 bfo, 6V6 af out AF OUT: 2 W. REMARKS: HRO-Jr built for US Navy. No crystal filter, "S" meter or bandspread.

MODEL: RAW YRS: WW II IF: 455 kHz FILTER: None TUBES: 9, 2 6D6 rf, 6C6 mix, 6C6 hfo, 2 6D6 if, 6B7 det/avc/af1, 6C6 bfo, 42 af out AF OUT: 1.5 W. REMARKS: Navy HRO-JR, no meter, bandspread or

NATIONAL

crystal filter.

MODEL: RBH BANDS: 0.3-1.2, 1.7-16 mHz REMARKS: Navy NC-100A with two RF stages. Ref: NC-156.

MODEL: RBJ YRS: WW II BANDS: 9, .05-.4, .48-30 mHz IF: 455 kHz FILTER: None TUBES: 9, 2 6D6 rf, 6C6 mix, 6C6 hfo, 2 6D6 if, 6B7 det/avc/af1, 6C6 bfo, 42 af out AF OUT: 1.5 W. REMARKS: Navy HRO-JR, no crystal filter, "S" meter or bandspread.

MODEL: RCE YRS: WW II TUBES: 9, 2 6D6 rf, 6C6 mix, 6C6 hfo, 2 6D6 if, 6B7 det/avc/af1, 6C6 bfo, 42 af out REMARKS: HRO-JR.

MODEL: RCK REMARKS: NC-100A.

MODEL: RCP REMARKS: FAA version of NC-100A.

MODEL: RCL YRS: WW-II REMARKS: Similar to NC-100

MODEL: URR-36 BANDS: 9, .05-35 mHz REMARKS: HRO-50.

MODEL: URR-39 BANDS: .05-30 mHz. REMARKS: No other information.

NATIONAL

MODEL: WRR-2 YRS: 1960-65 BANDS: 4, 2-32 mHz TYPE: Triple conversion, fixed HFO IF: 1625-1725, 220, 80 kHz FILTER: Crystal lattice TUBES: 64 plus 24 semi diodes, 32 5654, 5 5670, 5725, 7 5749, 65750, 3 5751, 2 5814A, 4 6005, 3 0B2WA, 12AT7WA, 4 1N198, 10 1N458, 2 1N457, 8 1N547 REMARKS: Replaces R-390A, synthesized HFO. See FRR-59.

MODEL: RHM REMARKS: Commercial designation for early AGS (q.v.)

MODEL: RHQ REMARKS: Commercial designation for early AGU (q.v.).

NORDEN

Norden Radio Laboratories, 315 Fourth Ave, New York, was the successor to the company which manufactured the famous Norden-Hauck broadcast receivers in the 1920's. H. L. Chadbourne visited their small office in late 1933 and met Alexander Norden, Jr, and was shown the "Navy" Model 34 and another small, bandswitching communications receiver about which nothing further is known. The Model 34 was obviously a Hammarlund Comet Pro with a couple of tuning meters added to the front panel. The significance of the use of "Navy" is not known. The model 34 was the subject of an article and advertisement in the January, 1934, Short Wave Craft which were the last known references to the receiver.

MODEL: Navy Model 34 YRS: 1933-34 BANDS: 5, .545-20 mHz FILTER: None IF: 465 kHz TUBES: 9, 57 mix, 58 hfo, 2 58 if, 57 det, 58 bfo, 2B7 avc amp/det, 2A5 af out, 80 rect AF OUT: 4 W. REMARKS: Same chassis as Comet Pro (Var 5), built by Hammarlund. Plug-in coils, two tuning meters.

PATTERSON

Emmitt Patterson started the Patterson Electric Company in 1919. The name was changed to Patterson Radio in the mid 1920's. The company hired Ray Gudie in 1933 and he designed their first communications receiver the All Wave 10 which became the PR-10. West Coast radio his-

PATTERSON

PATTERSON

torian Floyd Paul claims that up to 50,000 PR-10's were sold, mostly to Asia. If so, the PR-10 was one of the highest volume communications receivers in history.

Gudie left Patterson in 1934 when they were in the throes of developing the PR-12 which, although advertised and promoted, was never produced. Karl Pierson Pierson joined the company in 1934 and supervised the design of the PR-15 and PR-16. Pierson left in 1937 to start Pierson-DeLane and purchased Patterson's communications line including the PR-15.

Patterson went out of business in 1939. The company was located at 1320 So. Los Angeles St, Los Angeles, from 1931 to 1938 when it moved to 1612 West Pico Blvd. All of Patterson's chassis were manufactured by Gilfillan, Inc, under their RCA license at 1815 Venice Blvd, Los Angeles.

The PR-15 was tropic proofed, at least during its Paterson days, and large numbers were sold in the Far East, Indochina and China. Quite a switch from today! PR-15's were also used at the Los Angeles Times monitoring station for Amelia Earhart's last flight and reportedly picked up signals after she disappeared.

MODEL: All Wave 10 YRS: 1933 IF: 262 kHz REMARKS: Essentially same as PR-10. Differentiated by "Patterson All-Wave" marked on "R" meter.

Courtesy Hammond Museum of Radio

MODEL: PR-10 YRS: 1933-34 PRICE: $70.25 BANDS: 4, .54-21 mHz FILTER: None IF: 432.5 kHz TUBES: 10, 57 mix, 56 hfo, 3 58 if, 55 det/avc/af1, 57 bfo, 57 mtr amp, 59 af out, 5Z3 rect REMARKS: "R" meter, antenna trimmer, 50,000 reportedly sold, mostly in SE Asia.

MODEL: PR-12 (Prototype) YRS: 1934 PRICE: $83.70, $89.70 with crystal BANDS: 5, .55-32 mHz FILTER: Optional crystal TUBES: 12, 6D6 rf, 6A7 conv, 2 6D6 if, 75 det, 75 af1, 75 af2, 6D6 bfo, 6D6 mtr amp, 2 42 p/p af out, 5Z3 rect REMARKS: First announced October, 1934. In November, 1934, it was announced ". . .on August 7 [1934] all models [of the PR-12] submitted by the engineering staff were deliberately scrapped. That department has been reorganized and E. R. Patterson himself is now actively in charge as chief engineer." In the June, 1935, QST, "Now in production, The new improved Patterson PR-12 (Delivery during June)." No PR-12's were ever delivered.

MODEL: PR-12 Variation YRS: 1934-35 TUBES: 12, 6D6 rf, 6A7 conv, 3 6D6 if, 85 det/avc/af1, 6F7 "S"/mod mtr, 6D6 bfo, 76 af2, 2 42 p/p af out, 5Z3 rect REMARKS: This circuit variation shown in article and schematic in April, 1935, Radio.

PATTERSON

MODEL: PR-15 YRS: 1937-39 PRICE: $109.50
BANDS: 5, .55-40 mHz IF: 465 kHz FILTER:
Crystal TUBES: 15, 2 6K7 rf, 6A8 mix, 6K6
hfo, 6K7 if, 6L7 if/nl, 6Q7 det/avc/af1,
6K7 noise amp, 6H6 noise rect, 6N7 auto
threshold, 6J7 sq, 6C5 bfo, 2 6V6 af out,
5X4 rect AF OUT: 15 W.

MODEL: PR-16 YRS: 1935-36 PRICE: $89.70
BANDS: 5, .55-32 mHz IF: 458 kHz FILTER:
None TUBES: 16, 2 6D6 parallel rf, 6D6
mix, 6C6 hfo, 3 6D6 if, 6F7 det/bfo, 6C6
avc, 76 meter amp, 6A6 af inv, 2 76 af
driver, 2 6A3 af out, 5Z3 rect REMARKS:
Replaced PR-12, perhaps only communications receiver to use parallel rf amplifier tubes.

MODEL: PR-16 Variation REMARKS: Audio
output stage uses push-pull 42's.

MODEL: PR-16C PRICE: $95.70 FILTER:
Crystal REMARKS: PR-16 with crystal filter.

MODEL: PR-16CK, PR-16K REMARKS: Console
models of PR-16C and PR-16.

PATTERSON

MODEL: DeLuxe-16 YRS: 1938 PRICE: $69.50
BANDS: 4, .55-37 mHz FILTER: None RE-
MARKS: Last of the Patterson line, an all-
wave BC type receiver.

PHILMORE

Philmore Radio Co., was a manufacturer and distributor of low-priced accessories and components.

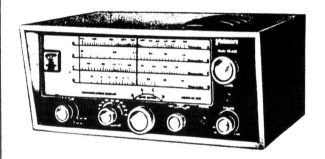

MODEL: CR-5AC YRS: 1961 PRICE: $51.90
BANDS: 4, .55-30 mHz FILTER: None TUBES:
4 + rect REMARKS: Internal speaker, probably imported.

PIERSON

Pierson Electronic Corp., 533 E. Fifth
St., Los Angeles, entered the post-war
market in 1946 with a top-of-the-line
communications receiver designed by Karl
E. Pierson of Patterson (q.v.) fame. This
was apparently their only product and
they went out of business in 1948. A rec-
ent issue of Electronic Radio said that
Pierson, W6BGH, had passed away at the
age of 83.

PIERSON

MODEL: KP-81 YRS: 1946-47 PRICE: $318
BANDS: 5, .54-40 mHz IF: 465 kHz FILTER:
Crystal TUBES: 20, 2 7A7 rf, 7B8 mix, 7B5
hfo, 7A7 if1, 6L7 if2, 7H7 if3, 7A4 inf imp
det, 7B4 af1, 7C7 bfo, 7Y4 avc, 7A6 noise
rect, 7H7 noise amp, 7A7 noise cont,
7A7 mtr amp, 7C7 sq, 7C7 calib, 2 7C5 af
out, 5U4 rect AF OUT: 12 W. REMARKS:
"Designed by Karl E. Pierson creator of
the PR series." Movable coil rack, cascaded if transformers, separate power
supply. Less than 300 built.

PIERSON-DELANE

Karl E. Pierson, W6BGH, and a Mr De-
Laplane (contracted to DeLane) formed
Pierson-DeLane, 2345-47 W. Washington
Blvd, Los Angeles, in 1937. The company
continued in business until 1943. Pierson
was president and chief engineer and
DeLaplane was VP and financial officer.
They purchased the communications equip-
ment line from Patterson Radio where
Pierson had designed the PR-15 and PR-16.
The PR-15 was modified slightly and was
Pierson-DeLane's major product until they
started concentrating on two-way radio
equipment in 1939. The receivers were
manufactured by Gilfillin Bros. (See Breting.)

MODEL: PR-15 YRS: 1937-39 REMARKS: Same
as Patterson PR-15 with minor design
changes. Over 2000 sold.

MODEL: PD-88 YRS: 1938-39 REMARKS: PR-15
in console cabinet. About 200 sold.

PIERSON-HOLT

Pierson-Holt Electronics, 2308 Washington Blvd, Venice, CA, was the last venture for Karl Pierson. The company exist-
ed from 1954-57 and they advertised their
receiver as the design of Karl E. Pierson
and as the successor to the KP-81.

The company was sold to Automation
Electronics, Inc, 1500 W. Verdugo Ave,
Burbank, CA, in 1957. They continued to
manufacture the KE-93 until 1960.

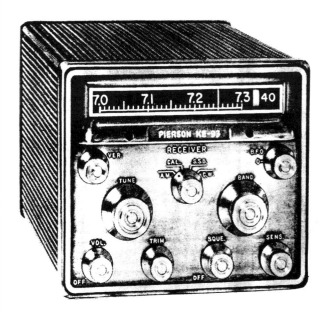

MODEL: KE-93 YRS: 1955-1960 PRICE:
$194.50 BANDS: 7, BC + 160-10 mtrs TYPE:
Double conversion, variable hfo IF: 2200,
265 kHz FILTER: 265 kHz L/C TUBES: 13,
6BZ6 rf, 6BE6 mix1, 3CB6 hfo, 6BE6 mix2/
xco, 6BA6 if1, 6BE6 if2, 6AL5 det/avc,
12AX7 af1/bfo, 6AU6 noise amp, 6AL5
noise rect/damp, 6BA8A sq, 6AQ5 af out,
7HTF ballast AF OUT: 3 W. REMARKS: Mobile type receiver, turret bandswitching, separate power supply.

POSTAL RADIO

Postal Radio Co., 133/135 Liberty St.,
New York City, produced communications
receivers and accessories in 1934 and
1935. S. Miller was chief engineer.

POSTAL RADIO

RCA

MODEL: International YRS: 1933-34 BANDS: .55-21 mHz IF: 465 kHz FILTER: None TUBES: 9, 57 rf, 57 mix, 58 hfo, 2 58 if, 57 det, 58 bfo, 2A5 af out, 80 rect AF OUT: 3 W. REMARKS: Triple gang plug-in coils which can be switched for either bandspread or general coverage. Originally sold as a kit.

MODEL: ACR-111 YRS: 1937-38 PRICE: $189 BANDS: 5, .54-32 mHz IF: 460 kHz FILTER: Crystal TUBES: 16, 2 6K7 rf, 6J7 mix, 6J7 hfo, 2 6K7 if, 6H6 det, 6E5 tun eye, 6C5 af1, 6J7 noise silencer, 6C5 af2, 6R7 avc, 6J7 bfo, 2 6F6 af out, 5Z3 rect AF OUT: 5 W.

MODEL: '35 YRS: 1934-35 BANDS: .55-23 mHz IF: 465 kHz FILTER: None TUBES: 10, 58 rf, 57 mix, 56 hfo, 2 58 if, 2B7 det/avc/ af1, 58 bfo, 2 2A5 af out, 80 rect REM-ARKS: Triple gang plug-in coils.

MODEL: ACR-136 YRS: 1934-35 PRICE: $69 BANDS: 3, .54-18 mHz IF: 460 kHz FILTER: None TUBES: 7, 6D6 rf, 6A7 conv, 6D6 if, 6B7 det/avc/af1, 6D6 bfo, 41 af out, 80 rect REMARKS: Internal speaker, airplane dial.

RCA

The RCA Victor Company, Inc., Amateur Radio Section, Camden, NJ, produced communications receivers from 1934 through World War II, culminating with the famous AR-88 and its variations which continued in production into the 1950's.

RCA

MODEL: ACR-155 YRS: 1936-38 PRICE: $74.50
BANDS: 3, .52-22 mHz IF: 460 kHz FILTER:
None TUBES: 9, 6K7 rf, 6L7 mix, 6J7 hfo,
6K7 if, 6H6 det/avc, 6F5 af1, 6J7 bfo, 6F6
af out, 5W4 rect AF OUT: 2 W. REMARKS:
Internal speaker.

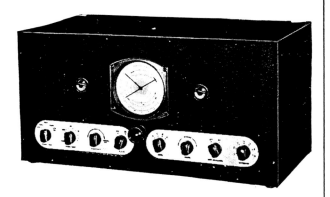

MODEL: ACR-175 YRS: 1936 PRICE: $119.50
BANDS: 4, .5-60 mHz IF: 460 kHz FILTER:
Crystal TUBES: 11, 6K7 rf, 6L7 mix, 6J7
hfo, 2 6K7 if, 6H6 det, 6F5 af1, 6J7 bfo,
6E5 eye, 6F6 af out, 5Z4 rect AF OUT: 4.5
W. REMARKS: Tuning eye, airplane dial.

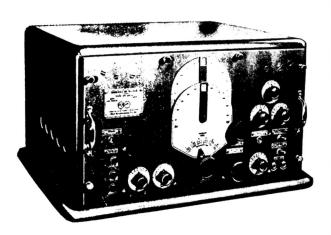

MODEL: AR-60 (R-T-S) YRS: 1935-36 PRICE:
$495 IF: 750 kHz FILTER: Crystal TUBES:
11, 2 6C6 rf, 6C6 mix, 6C6 hfo, 2 6D6 if,
6B7 det/avc, 6F7 bfo/af1, 41 af out, 991
vr, rect REMARKS: Weighed over 70 lbs,
antenna matching circuit matches 50-500
ohms. R suffix = rack model, T = black
table model, S = two tone gray table model.

MODEL: AR-77 YRS: 1940-41 PRICE: $139.50
BANDS: 6, .54-31 mHz FILTER: Crystal
TUBES: 10 AF OUT: 3 W.

MODEL: AR-88 YRS: 1941-45 BANDS: 6, .535-
32 mHz IF: 455 kHz FILTER: Crystal TUBES:
14, 2 6SG7 rf, 6SA7 mix, 6J5 hfo, 3 6SG7
if, 6H6 det/avc, 6H6 nl, 6SJ7 af1, 6J5 bfo,
6K6 af out, VR-150 vr, 5Y3 rect AF OUT:
2.5 W. REMARKS: Electrical design by Les-
ter T. Fowler, mechanical design by
George Blaker. No crystal phasing control. Most of production sold to England
during World War II.

MODEL: AR-88D REMARKS: "D" = desk, i.e.,
with cabinet.

MODEL: AR-88LF BANDS: 6, .125-.55, 1.5-30
mHz IF: 735 kHz REMARKS: Low frequency
model.

RCA

MODEL: ARB YRS: WW II BANDS: 4, .195-9.05 mHz IF: 135 kHz bands 1&2 (.195-1.6 mHz), 915 kHz bands 3&4 FILTER: None TUBES: 6, 12SF7 rf, 12SA7 conv, 12SF7 if1, 12SF7 if2/det, 12SF7 bfo/avc, 12A6 af out REMARKS: Navy aircraft receiver. 30,000 manufactured. 24 V. dynamotor power supply. Reference also CRV-46457, CRV-46151.

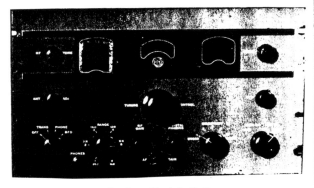

Courtesy Electric Radio

MODEL: CR-88 YRS: 1940's REMARKS: AR-88 with smooth, gray panel and addition of crystal phasing control. AF gain, RF gain and crystal phasing form a triangle under the main tuning knob.

MODEL: CR-88A REMARKS: CR-88 configured as a component of the DR-89A triple diversity receiver unit.

MODEL: CR-88B YRS: 1951-? BANDS: 6, .535-32 mHz IF: 455 kHz FILTER: Crystal TUBES: 16, 2 6SG7 rf, 6SA7 mix, 6J5 hfo, 3 6SG7 if, 6H6 det/avc, 6H6 nl, 6J5 bfo, 6J5 xtal cal, 6SL7 af1/inv, 2 6K6 p/p af out, VR-150 vr, 5U4 rect REMARKS: Built for RCA Radiomarine Corp. Single band-in-use dial, provisons for crystal control, 500 kHz crystal calibrator, 3 position selectivity control.

MODEL: CR-91 YRS: 1944-? BANDS: 6, .073-.55, 1.48-30.5 IF: 735 kHz TUBES: Same as AR-88 except 6V6 af out replaces 6K6. REMARKS: AR-88 series, smooth gray front panel and crystal phasing control as in CR-88 (q.v.).

MODEL: CR-91A REMARKS: Differences not known.

MODEL: CRV-46151 REMARKS: See ARB

MODEL: CRV-46246 REMARKS: Navy AR-88

MODEL: CRV-46457 REMARKS: See ARB.

MODEL: DR-89 REMARKS: Triple diversity receiver with three AR-88 each with a diversity control in lower right of front panel. Housed in 6 ft rack.

MODEL: MI-17091A REMARKS: Same as CR-91.

MODEL: OA-58A/FRC YRS: 1947-? REMARKS: Triple diversity receiver with three R-320 receivers (SC-88).

MODEL: R-320 REMARKS: Signal Corps designation for SC-88.

MODEL: RBB-1 thru -6 YRS: WW II BANDS: 0.5-4 mHz IF: 400 kHz FILTER: None TUBES: 19 including power supply, 2 6SK7 rf, 6AB7 mix, 6AB7 hfo, 3 6SK7 if, 6AB7 bfo, 6H6 det/avc, 6H6 nl/out lim, 6SK7 af1, 6SK7 out lim amp, 6H6 sil/out lim, 6AB7 af2, 6K6 af out, 991 volt lim, 6-8B ballast, OC3 vr, 5U4 rect REMARKS: USN shipboard receiver. Also manufactured by Federal Telephone.

MODEL: RBC-1 thru -6 YRS: WW II BANDS: 4, 4-27 mHz TUBES: Same as RBB except 6AB7 rf1. REMARKS: Same as RBB except frequency coverage and first RF tube.

MODEL: RBC-3a REMARKS: 400 Hz version.

RCA

MODEL: RDM-1 REMARKS: Triple diversity receiver consisting of three CRV-46246B each with a diversity control in the lower right of front panel.

MODEL: SC-88 REMARKS: AR-88 series with black crackle panel, crystal phasing, single band-in-use dial, some with diversity control.

MODEL: AN/URR-2 BANDS: 14, .014-32 mHz REMARKS: No further info.

RME

Radio Manufacturing Engineers of Peoria, Ill., was a small company that made a big name for itself in the amateur communications receiver field. They had their peak recognition during the 1930's when they were one of the pioneers in the receiver market along with National Hallicrafters and Hammarlund.

The company was started in 1931/32 by E. G. Shalkhauser, W9CI, and Russ M. Planck, W9RGH. The first receiver, the RME-9 was designed in 1932 and only about 100 were manufactured in W9CI's cellar. The receiver was redesigned to the RME-9D in 1934.

The company moved to a storefront at 313-315 Bradley Ave., in 1934 and in 1935 moved again to a factory at 306 First Ave., where they remained for many years.

Their most popular model, the RME-69 was introduced in 1935 and 6500 were manufactured through 1940. The -69 was followed in 1940 by the RME-41, -43 and -99 all of which resembled , electrically and physically, the post-war RME-45. These later receivers never attained the popularity of the -69.

RME was a small company, employing no more than 120 people even during its peak while manufacturing instruments during World War II. It was a sharply focused company.

RME

The company was not a big success after the war and finally merged with Electro-Voice in 1953. Shalkhauser left the company then but Planck stayed on to supervise the design of a new series of receivers. RME remained in Peoria for awhile but was later consolidated with other Electro-Voice operations in Buchanon, Mich. During the Electro-Voice days RME produced the 4300, 4350, 6900 and 6902 receivers but they never recaptured the glory of the 1930's.

In 1962 G. C. Electronics of Rockford, Ill., purchased RME but the RME name disappeared within a year.

MODEL: RME-9 YRS: 1932-33 PRICE: $106.50 BANDS: 5, .54-22 mHz IF: 500 kHz FILTER: Crystal TUBES: 9, 58 rf, 57 mix, 58 hfo, 2 58 if, 2B7 det/avc/af1, 24A bfo, 2A5 af out, 80 rect REMARKS: Single airplane dial, "R" meter. Less than 100 built.

MODEL: RME-9D YRS: 1934-35 PRICE: $112.50 BANDS: 5, .54-22 mHz IF: 465 kHz FILTER: Crystal TUBES: 9, 58 rf, 57 mix, 58 hfo, 2 58 if, 2B7 det/avc/af1, 24A bfo, 2A5 af out, 80 rect REMARKS: Twin airplane dials with "R" meter between them. Included antenna trimmer and "R" meter calibrated in "R" units and microvolts.

MODEL: RME-9D Special BANDS: 5, 1.45-32 mHz REMARKS: Otherwise same as standard -9D.

MODEL: ME-14 YRS: 1939 BANDS: 0.18-4.1 mHz TUBES: 6 REMARKS: Battery operated portable.

MODEL: RME-41 YRS: 1941-45 PRICE: $94.50 BANDS: 6, .54-33 mHz IF: 455 kHz FILTER: None TUBES: 9, 7B7 rf, 7J7 conv, 2 7B7 if, 7B6 det/bfo, 7C7 af1, 7A6 anl/avc, 7C5 af out, 80 rect AF OUT: 3 W. REMARKS: RME-43 without crystal filter and "S" meter.

MODEL: RME-43 YRS: 1941-45 PRICE: $109.50 FILTER: Crystal REMARKS: Same as RME-41 with addition of crystal filter and "S" meter.

MODEL: RME-45 YRS: 1945-47 PRICE: $166 BANDS: 6, .50-33 mHz IF: 455 kHz FILTER: Crystal TUBES: 9, 7B7 rf, 7J7 conv, 2 7B7 if, 7B6 det/bfo, 7C7 af1, 7A6 nl, 7C5 af out, 80 rect

MODEL: RME-45B YRS: 1947-48 BANDS: 6, .55-33 mHz IF: 455 kHz FILTER: Crystal TUBES: 10, 7B7 rf, 7J7 conv, 2 7B7 if, 7B6 det/bfo, 7C7 af1, 7A6 nl, 7C5 af out, VR-150 vr, 80 rect REMARKS: Changes from RME-45: two speed tuning, calibrated band spread, VR-150, improved noise limiter with on/off switch.

MODEL: RME-49 REMARKS: No data available.

MODEL: RME-50 YRS: 1952-53 PRICE: $187.50 BANDS: 6, .54-33 mHz IF: 455 kHz FILTER: Crystal TUBES: 12, 6BA6 rf, 6U8 mix/hfo, 2 6BA6 if, 6AL5 det/anl, 6AU6 af1, 6AU6 bfo, 6BA6 fm lim, 6AL5 ratio det, 6V6 af out, VR-150 vr, 5Y3 rect AF OUT: 3 W. REMARKS: Manual shows 6BA6 rf and if amplifiers on schematic and 6BJ6 in tube list. Earlier models may have used loctal tubes. Essentially the same circuit as RME-45B with addition of plug-in NBFM adaptor.

MODEL: RME-50A REMARKS: Differences between -50 and -50A not known.

MODEL: RME-55 REMARKS: No data available.

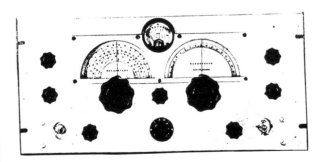

MODEL: RME-69 YRS: 1935-40 PRICE: $134.90 BANDS: 6, .55-32 mHz IF: 465 kHz FILTER: Crystal TUBES: 9, 6D6 rf, 6C6 mix, 2 6D6 if, 6B7 det/avc/af1, 6D6 bfo, 42 af out, 80 rect AF OUT: 2.6 W. REMARKS: 6500 built.

MODEL: RME-69/LS-1 TUBES: 11, replaces 2 6D6 if with 6L7 if1, 6K7 if2, 6J7 noise amp, 6H6 noise rect REMARKS: Includes factory installed LS-1 noise suppressor. The bfo switch is changed from lower right corner to lower left under phone jack. The silencer control is in lower right corner.

MODEL: RME-69/Battery REMARKS: Battery model operates from either A. C. or batterys. Battery switch located lower left corner under phone jack.

MODEL: RME-69/LS-1/Battery REMARKS: Battery model with LS-1 installed. Silencer control is in lower right with BFO switch under it and battery switch in s lower left under phone jack.

MODEL: RME-69/DB-20 TUBES: 12, adds 2 6K7 rf, 80 rect REMARKS: RME-69 and DB-20 preselector built into same cabinet.

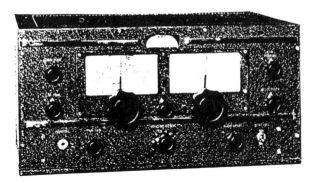

MODEL: RME-70 YRS: 1938-40 PRICE: $138.60 BANDS: 6, .55-32 mHz IF: 465 kHz FILTER: Crystal TUBES: 11, 6K7 rf, 6J7 mix, 6K7 hfo, 2 6K7 if, 6H6 det/avc, 6K7 af1, 6H6 nl, 6K7 bfo, 6F6 af out, 80 rect REMARKS: "Resonator" control, 2 gang trimmer, Dickert noise limiter.

MODEL: RME-70/DB-20 TUBES: 14, adds 2 6K7 rf, 80 rect REMARKS: RME-70 and DB-20 built into same cabinet.

MODEL: RME-70/DM-36 REMARKS: RME-70 and DM-36 28-60 mHz converter in same cabinet.

MODEL: RME-79 YRS: 1953-54 PRICE: $287 BANDS: 6, .54-30 mHz FILTER: Crystal TUBES: 12, 2 6BA6 rf, 6BE6 mix, 6C4 hfo, 2 6BA6 if, 6AU6 bfo, 6AL5 det/anl, 6AV6 af1, 6AQ5 af out, VR-150 vr, 5Y3 rect REMARKS: "Dial-O-Matic" tuning. Provisions for optional plug-in SSB adaptor.

RME

MODEL: RME-84 YRS: 1946-48 PRICE: $98.70
BANDS: 4, .54-44 mHz IF: 455 kHz FILTER:
None TUBES: 8, 7B7 rf, 7S7 conv, 2 7B7 if,
7K7 det/avc/af1, 7K7 nl/bfo, 6G6 af out,
5Y3 rect AF OUT: 1.1 W. REMARKS: Internal speaker.

MODEL: RME-84A REMARKS: Differences
not known.

MODEL: RME-99 YRS: 1940-41 PRICE: $137.40
BANDS: 6, .54-33 mHz IF: 465 kHz FILTER:
Crystal TUBES: 12, 7A7 rf, 7B8 mix, 7A4
hfo, 3 7A7 if, 7F7 det/af1, 7A4 bfo, 7A6
avc/anl, 7C5 af out, VR-150 vr, 80 rect
AF OUT: 4 W. REMARKS: First of the RME-
45 look-alike series.

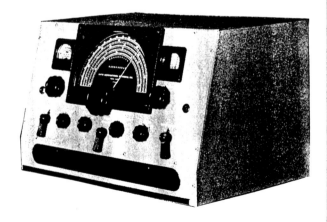

MODEL: RME-99 Deluxe YRS: 1941 PRICE:
$139.65 REMARKS: Sloping panel cabinet
with blank space at bottom for transmitter controls.

RME

MODEL: RME 4300 YRS: 1955-57 PRICE: $194
BANDS: 6 ham bands, 160-10 mtrs IF: 455
kHz FILTER: Crystal TUBES: 8, 6CB6 rf,
6U8 mix/hfo, 6CB6 if1, 6U8 af2/bfo, 6T8
det/anl/af1, 6AQ5 af out, 0A2 vr, 5Y3 rect

MODEL: RME 4350 YRS: 1957 PRICE: $229
BANDS: 6 ham bands, 160-10 mtrs TYPE:
Double conversion, tunable HFO IF: 2195,
455 kHz FILTER: Crystal TUBES: 9, 6BZ6 rf,
6U8 mix1/hfo, 6U8 mix2/xco, 6CB6 if1, 6U8
if2/bfo, 6T8 det/anl/af1, 6AQ5 af out, 0A2
vr, 5Y3 rect AF OUT: 1.5 W.

MODEL: RME 4350A YRS: 1957-59 PRICE: $249
TUBES: 10, as 4350 except adds 6CB6 calib
REMARKS: Same as 4350 except adds crys-
tal calibrator.

RME

MODEL: RME 6900 YRS: 1959-62 PRICE: $349
BANDS: 6, WWV + 5 ham bands, 80-10 mtrs
TYPE: Double conversion, tunable hfo
IF: 2195, 57 kHz FILTER: 57 kHz L/C
TUBES: 12 + 2 Si Rect, 6BA6 rf, 6U8 mix1/
hfo, 6U8 mix2/xco, 6C4 if1, 2 6BA6 if2/3,
6AL5 if nl, 6T8 det/avc/af1, 12AT7 prod
det/bfo, 6CB6 calib, 6AQ5 af out, 2 1N1763
rect AF OUT: 1 W. REMARKS: Ad says,
"engineered under the supervision of Russ
Planck, W9RGH" and "its extraordinary
namesake, the world famous RME-69, the
first bandswitching receiver ever produced." The latter statement was far
from true!

MODEL: RME 6902 YRS: 1960-61 PRICE: $249
BANDS: 5 ham bands, 80-10 mtrs FILTER:
Crystal TUBES: 12 AF OUT: 1.5 W.

ROSS

A. H. Ross & Co. produced several communications receivers from 1933 through
1935. They were originally located at 5839
Germantown Ave in Philadelphia and late
at Keswick Ave. and Waverly Road in
Glenside, PA. Their first receiver, the 2B,
was originally described in an article in
the August, 1933, QST.

ROSS

MODEL: 2B YRS: 1933 PRICE: $70 BANDS: 2*
IF: 465 kHz FILTER: None TUBES: 6, 2A7
conv, 2 58 if, 2A7 det/bfo, 47 af out, 80
rect REMARKS: *Bandswitching for any two
selected ham bands.

MODEL: Jupiter YRS: 1934 PRICE: $49.50
BANDS: 4 REMARKS: Appears same as 2B
electrically with added bands and new
look.

ROSS

MODEL: 4-C Special YRS: 1935 BANDS: 4, .55-20 mHz FILTER: None TUBES: 8, 6D6 rf, 6A7 conv, 2 6D6 if, 6B7 det/avc/af1, 6D6 bfo, 42 af out, 80 rect

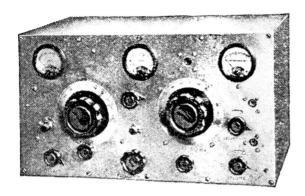

MODEL: Unknown YRS: 1935 REMARKS: Three meters!!

SARGENT

The E. M. Sargent Co., 212 Ninth St., Oakland, CA, produced communications receivers from 1933 to 1940 and an affiliated company, Radio Constructors Co., produced a couple of embryonic communications receivers as early as 1930 and 1931.

E. M Sargent and L. G. Rayment formed Radio Service Co. at 1200 Franklin St., Oakland in 1922. They ran a radio store in the storefront and had a workshop in the basement where they developed a number of BC receivers. In 1924 Sargent formed E. M. Sargent Co. in his home at 721 McKinley, Oakland. It is not clear what the company did until it began producing communications receivers in 1933. In 1927 Radio Service Co. split into Radio Constructors Co., 357 Twelth St., and Pioneer Radio Co., which remained at 1200 Franklin St. The latter then merged into Radio Constructors Co. which moved to 3714 San Pablo in 1931 and then folded in the same year.

Sargent was an old shipboard radio operator and his company specialized in marine receivers and made a number of marine and ham regenerative receivers in addition to their superhets. In 1934 E. M.

SARGENT

Sargent moved to 212 Ninth St. where they remained for the rest of their existence. They made their last general communications receiver in 1940. In 1948 Sargent sold his stock to long time associate L. C. Rayment who, with his son Will, formed Sargent-Rayment Co. to manufacture high-fidelity equipment. E. M. Sargent died in 1948 at the age of 56.

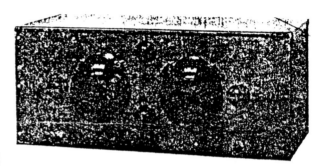

MODEL: Long-Distance De Luxe YRS: 1930 TUBES: 11 REMARKS: "Static reducer", battery operated. Built by affiliate company Radio Constructors Co.

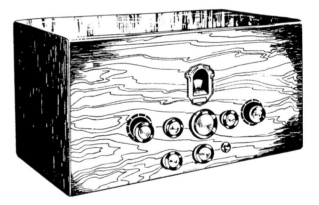

MODEL: Amateur Special YRS: 1931 BANDS: 1.5-30 mHz REMARKS: Band switch, bandspread, push-pull pentode af output. Built by affiliate company Radio Constructors

SARGENT

MODEL: 8-34 YRS: 1934-35 PRICE: $49.50
BANDS: 4, .55-21 mHz IF: 465 kHz FILTER:
None TUBES: 8, 57 mix, 57 hfo, 2 58 if,
56 det, 56 bfo, 2A5 af out, 80 rect.
REMARKS: Used an antenna trimmer.

MODEL: 8-34 Marine PRICE: $57.50 BANDS:
5, 0.2-20 mHz REMARKS: Otherwise same
as standard 8-34.

MODEL: 8-34 Europa Model BANDS: 5, 0.2-
20 mHz REMARKS: No other information.

MODEL: 9-33 YRS: 1933-34 PRICE: $69.50
BANDS: 4 IF: 465, 175 kHz TYPE: Double
conversion, tunable hfo FILTER: None
TUBES: 9, 57 mix, 57 hfo, 2A7 conv, 58 if,
56 det, 57 bfo, 2 2A5 af out, 80 rect REM-
ARKS: First double conversion receiver?
Bandspread accomplished by swivelling the
stator of the tuning capacitor.

MODEL: All-Wave Explorer YRS: 1934 PRICE:
$69.50 BANDS: .55-23 mHz TUBES: 9 REM-
ARKS: Internal speaker.

SARGENT

MODEL: 20MA YRS: 1935-36 PRICE: $67.50
BANDS: 5, 0.2-21 mHz IF: 525 kHz FILTER:
None TUBES: 9, 6D6 rf, 6C6 mix, 6C6 hfo,
2 6D6 if, 76 det, 42 af out, 80 rect REM-
ARKS: Marine model.

MODEL: 20SA PRICE: $59.50 BANDS: 4, .55-
21 mHz REMARKS: Standard model - same
as 20MA except price and eliminates LW
band.

MODEL: 20XSA PRICE: $64.50 BANDS: 5, .55-
30 mHz REMARKS: 20SA with added 10
meter band.

MODEL: 21-AA YRS: 1936-37 PRICE: $139
BANDS: 5, .55-30 mHz IF: 535 kHz FILTER:
None TUBES: 12, 6K7 rf, 6J7 rf regen, 6L7
mix, 6J7 hfo, 2 6K7 if, 6C5 det, 6J7 bfo,
6J7 avc, 6E5 tun eye, 6F6 af out, 5Z3 rect
REMARKS: Regenerative RF using separate
regeneration tube.

MODEL: 21-MA YRS: 1936-37 PRICE: $155
BANDS: 7, .08-30 mHz TUBES: 12 REMARKS:
Regenerative RF stage.

MODEL: 21A REMARKS: No details available.

SARGENT

MODEL: Streamliner 39 YRS: 1938-39 PRICE: $33.90 BANDS: 4, .55-31 mHz FILTER: None TUBES: 5, 6K8 conv, 6F7 if/bfo, 75 det/avc/af1, 42 af out, 80 rect REMARKS: Internal speaker. Ad says "2 if" stages?

MODEL: Streamliner 39 (Battery Model) PRICE: $38.90 REMARKS: No other info.

MODEL: WAC-44 YRS: 1940 PRICE: $139 BANDS: 5, .54-31 mHz IF: 456 kHz FILTER: Crystal TUBES: 11, 2 6K7 rf, 6L7 mix, 6J7 hfo, 6K7 if1, 6F7 1f2/mtr amp, 6H6 det/avc, 6F7 af1/bfo/calib, 6F6 af out, VR-150 vr, 80 rect REMARKS: Internal speaker, panel trimmers for the two RF stages.

MODEL: 50 YRS: 1938 PRICE: $127 BANDS: 6, .15-.4, .54-23 mHz TUBES: 8, incl. rf, conv, 2 if, det/af1, 6E5 eye, 2 43 af out, 80 rect REMARKS: Internal speaker, AC/DC.

SARGENT

MODEL: 51-AK YRS: 1938-40 PRICE: $157 BANDS: 5, .54-31 mHz IF: 535 kHz FILTER: None TUBES: 10, 6F7 rf/regen, 6L7 mix, 6K7 hfo, 6F7 if1/if2, 6Q7 det/af1/avc, 6E5 tun eye, 6C5 bfo, 2 25L6 p/p af out, 80 rect AF OUT: 5 W. REMARKS: Internal speaker, AC/DC, RF and mixer panel trimmers. Triode section of 6F7 used as a feedback element to provide RF regeneration (RF Q Multiplier).

MODEL: 51-MK PRICE: $175 BANDS: 7, .08-31 mHz REMARKS: Marine version.

SCOTT

E. H. Scott, a native New Zealander, came to the United States after World War I. He founded the Scott Transformer Co., in 1924. The name of the company was changed in 1931 to Scott Radio Labs and was located at 4470 Ravenswood Ave., Chicago.

Scott Radio Labs was the best known of the manufacturers of custom, high-end broadcast receivers who flourished during the 1930's. Scott peaked in popularity in 1937 with the introduction of the massive, chrome plated 30 tube Philharmonic model. It was modestly proclaimed in full-page ads as "World's Most Powerful Radio".

Just prior to World War II Scott produced a limited run of a special 26 tube communications receiver. During the war he produced specially shielded, low radiation receivers for shipboard use for both communications and entertainment.

SCOTT

Scott sold most of his interest in the company in 1944 and resigned in 1945 after finding himself demoted from president to sales manager. He died in his retirement home in Victoria, BC, Canada,

Meanwhile, the company became unprofitable by 1947 after entering the TV business. It was sold in 1950 to John S. Meck and had a brief revival of profitability in 1951 but by 1956 was bankrupt. The Scott Radio Labs name was exploited by a couple of companies until 1961 when it died forever as the result of a suit by H. H. Scott, Inc.

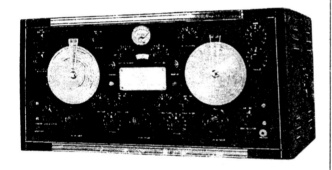

MODEL: Special Communications Receiver YRS: 1940-41 PRICE: $650 BANDS: 9, .14-64 mHz FILTER: Crystal TUBES: 26, 2 6U7 rf, 6L7 mix, 6J5 hfo (BC & LW tuner 2 6U7 rf, 6L7 mix, 6J5 hfo), 3 6K7 if, 6B8 avc amp/ det, 6B8 det/bfo, 6K7 af1, 6J5 ph inv, 2 6J5 af drive, 6B8 & 6J7 static & scratch sup, 6J5 mtr amp, 6H6 nl, 2 6L6 af out,

SIGMON

Sigmon Radio Supply Co., 104 Washington St., East, Charleston, W. Va., briefly entered the communications receiver market in 1940. They offered a receiver designed by Harry Hooten, W8KPX, a popular radio writer of the day.

SIGMON

MODEL: W8KPX Receiver YRS: 1940 BANDS: 5 ham bands, 80-5 mtrs IF: 1600 kHz FILTER: None TUBES: 10, 1232 rf, 7J7 mix, 7B7 hfo, 2 7A7 if, 6H6 det/avc/nl, 6C5 af1, 7B7 bfo, 7C5 af out, 5Y4 rect REMARKS: Kit. Plug-in coils.

SILVERTONE

The giant mail-order house, Sears, Roebuck & Co., offered a couple of house brand communications receivers during the 1930's.

MODEL: Silvertone Super-Eight YRS: 1936 PRICE: $49.95 BANDS: 3, .54-18 mHz TUBES: 8 REMARKS: Internal speaker.

SILVERTONE

MODEL: Silvertone Precision <u>YRS:</u> 1939 <u>PRICE:</u> $94.50 <u>BANDS:</u> 6, .54-65 mHz <u>FILTER:</u> Crystal <u>TUBES:</u> 12 <u>REMARKS:</u> Appears to be a repackaged Howard 450A.

SONAR

Sonar Radio Corp., 59 Myrtle Ave. (later 3050 West 21st St.), Brooklyn, NY, manufactured mobile-type receivers in 1952-53.

MODEL: MR-3 <u>YRS:</u> 1952-53 <u>PRICE:</u> $89.95 <u>BANDS:</u> 3 ham bands, 10-11, 20, 75 mtrs <u>IF:</u> 500 kHz <u>FILTER:</u> None <u>TUBES:</u> 8, 12AT7 rf/bfo, 12AT7 conv, 2 6BA6 if, 6AL5 det/ nl, 6AT6 af1, 6AQ5 af out, 0B2 vr <u>AF OUT:</u> 4.5 W. <u>REMARKS:</u> Mobile-type, separate power supply.

MODEL: MR-4 <u>YRS:</u> 1952-53 <u>PRICE:</u> $89.95 <u>BANDS:</u> 3 ham bands, 20, 40, 75/80 mtrs <u>REMARKS:</u> Same as MR-3 except freq.

SQUIRES-SANDERS

Squires-Sanders, 475 Watchung Ave., Watchung, NJ, manufactured a high dynamic range receiver designed by William Squires using a technique described by him in a popular <u>QST</u> article, "A New Approach to Receiver Front-End Design."

MODEL: SS-1BS <u>YRS:</u> 1967 <u>PRICE:</u> $1200 <u>REMARKS:</u> SS-1R with shortwave BC coverage.

MODEL: SS-1R <u>YRS:</u> 1963-66 <u>PRICE:</u> $895 <u>BANDS:</u> 10 + 2 fix tune WWV, 80-10 mtrs <u>TYPE:</u> Double conversion, fixed hfo <u>IF:</u> 5000-5500, 1000 kHz <u>FILTER:</u> Crystal lattice <u>TUBES:</u> 12 + 10 semi diodes, 7360 mix1, 6BH6 xco, 7360 mix2, 6BK7 vfo/k fol, 2 6BA6 if, 6AX8 if3/af1, 6AL5 nl, 6AL5 agc, 6BE6 prod det, 6AU6 bfo, 6AS5 af out, 1N34A det, 2 1N34A vfo shift, 1N34A agc clamp/delay, 3 1N34A bfo sw, 3 SD-4 rect <u>AF OUT:</u> 1 W.

SQUIRES-SANDERS

MODEL: SS-1R/701 YRS: 1966-67 REMARKS: Changes from SS-1R: 6BY6 prod det, 6AV6 if k fol, crystal bfo, better sensitivity, improved reliability, better dial drum and display system.

SWAN

Swan Electronics, 305 Airport Road, Oceanside, CA, was founded in 1960 by Herb Johnson (W8QKI, W6QKI, W7GRA) in Benson, AZ. They introduced their first product, a single band SSB transceiver, in May, 1961. The transceiver sold for $275 at a time when the Collins KWM-2 went for $1150. Business boomed and moved to a new plant in Oceanside in June, 1962. During their later days they offered a separate receiver/transmitter package.

MODEL: 600-R YRS: 1971-73 PRICE: $395 BANDS: 5 ham bands, 80-10 mtrs IF: 5500 kHz FILTER: Crystal lattice TUBES: 7 + 8 transistors + 12 semi diodes, 6BZ6 rf, 6BZ6

SWAN

mix, 2N706 hfo, 2N706 hfo buff, 2 2N706 isol amp, 2 12BA6 if, 2N706 bfo, 12AX7 prod det/af1, 12AV6 avc amp/rect, 6AQ5 af out, 4 MPS3693 calib AF OUT: 3 W.

MODEL: 600-R Custom PRICE: $545.95 TUBES: 9 + 8 transistors + 13 semi diodes, same as 600-R except adds 2 12BA6 noise amp, 1 noise rect diode, 1 IC af filter. REMARKS: Same as 600-R with addition of IC audio peak/notch filter and IF noise blanker.

MODEL: 600-R Custom/SS-16B REMARKS: Same as 600-R Custom with addition of special 16 pole filter.

TMC

Technical Materiel Corp., 700 Fenimore Road, Mamaroneck, NY, founded by Ray H. DePasquale, was a prominent manufacturer of military communications equipment during the 1950's and -60's.

MODEL: DDR-3 REMARKS: Diversity system using GPR-90 receivers.

MODEL: GPR-D REMARKS: GPR-90 for diversity applications. Provisions for external control of HFO, BFO, IFO.

MODEL: GPR-90 YRS: 1955-56 PRICE: $395 BANDS: 6, .54-31 mHz TYPE: Double conversion, tunable hfo IF: 3955, 455 kHz FILTER: Crystal TUBES: 15, 6AB4 rf1, 6CB6 rf2, 6AU6 mix, 6AG5 hfo, 6BE6 mix2/xco, 6BA6 if buf, 3 6BA6 if, 6AL5 det/nl, 6AG5 bfo, 12AX7 avc/af1, 6V6 af out, 0A2 vr,

5U4 rect <u>AF OUT:</u> 2 W. <u>REMARKS:</u> Military R-825/URR.

<u>MODEL:</u> GPR-90 (Variation) <u>YRS:</u> 1956-62 <u>PRICE:</u> $495 <u>TUBES:</u> 16, adds 6AU6 calib to original GPR-90 <u>REMARKS:</u> Original GPR-90 with addition of crystal calibrator. Calibrator switch located to left of range selector.

<u>MODEL:</u> GPR-90RX <u>REMARKS:</u> GPR-90 with addition of ten crystal controlled frequencies and a rear HFO/synthesizer input. Military R-840URR.

<u>MODEL:</u> GPR-91RXD <u>REMARKS:</u> GPR-90RXD with 15 kHz bandpass for four channel independent sideband reception.

<u>MODEL:</u> GPR-92 <u>YRS:</u> 1963-64 <u>BANDS:</u> 6, .54-32 mHz <u>TYPE:</u> Double conversion, tunable HFO <u>FILTER:</u> Crystal <u>TUBES:</u> 18 + 5 semi diodes, 6DC6 rf1, 6BA6 rf2, 6AH6 iso amp, 6BA7 mix1, 6AH6 hfo, 6AU6 hfo, 6U8 mix2/xco, 2 6BA6 if, 6AL5 nl, 6CB6 calib,

6AZ8 if/sq, 6U8 avc amp/det, 12AT7 prod det/bfo, 6AB4 vfo amp, 12AT7 af1/af driver, 6AQ5 af out, OB2 vr, 2 1N1084 rect, 2 1N34 rect, 1N463 rect <u>REMARKS:</u> Features 6 dB noise figure.

<u>MODEL:</u> GPR-92S <u>REMARKS:</u> Rack mounted model.

<u>MODEL:</u> R-825/URR <u>REMARKS:</u> See GPR-90.

<u>MODEL:</u> R-840/URR <u>REMARKS:</u> See GPR-90RX.

TOBE

The Tobe Deutschmann Corp., Canton, MA, offered a line of kit receivers during the mid-1930's. The receivers were designed by Glen Browning of Browning-Drake fame. The kits used the pre-assembled Tobe Tuner. Founder Tobe Deutschman died in 1991 at the age of 94.

<u>MODEL:</u> H (Standard) <u>YRS:</u> 1935-36 <u>PRICE:</u> $41.40 <u>BANDS:</u> 4 ham bands, 160-20 mtrs <u>IF:</u> 456 kHz <u>FILTER:</u> Regenerative IF <u>TUBES:</u> 7, 6D6 rf, 6A7 conv, 6D6 if, 75 det/avc/af1, 76 bfo, 42 af out, 80 rect <u>REMARKS:</u> Triple tuned IF transformers. First ham band only receiver?

<u>MODEL:</u> H (Special) <u>PRICE:</u> $47.40 <u>REMARKS:</u> Same as standard model except uses air trimmers vs mica trimmers in the tuner.

TOBE

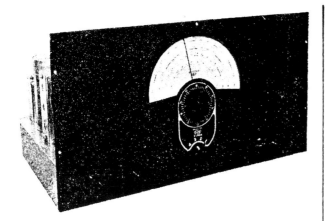

MODEL: Browning 35 (2.5 V. version) YRS: 1935 BANDS: 4, .55-22.6 mHz IF: 465 kHz FILTER: None TUBES: 7, 58 rf, 2A7 conv, 58 if, 2A6 det/af1, 56 bfo, 2A5 af out, 80 rect REMARKS: Kit. Triple tuned IF transformers.

MODEL: Browning 35 (6.3 V. version) YRS: 1935 TUBES: 7, 6D6 rf, 6A7 conv, 6D6 if, 75 det/af1, 76 bfo, 42 af out, 80 rect

MODEL: Browning 35 (Metal tube version) YRS: 1936 IF: 456 kHz TUBES: 8, 6K7 rf, 6A8 conv, 6K7 if, 6H6 det, 6F5 af1, 6C5 bfo, 6F6 af out, 80 rect.

MISC

During 1934 and 1935 a group of eleven component manufacturers sponsored the design of two low priced communications receivers for home construction which were featured in articles and advertisements in all the popular radio magazines.

MISC

MODEL: All-Star YRS: 1934 BANDS: 6, .55-30 mHz IF: 370 kHz FILTER: None TUBES: 6, 2A7 conv, 2 58 if, 56 det, 2A5 af out, 5Z3 rect. REMARKS: Kit. Plug-in coils.

MODEL: All-Star, Jr. YRS: 1935 PRICE: $27.97 BANDS: 6, .54-30 mHz IF: 370 kHz FILTER: None TUBES: 5, 6A7 conv, 6F7 if, 77 det, 42 af out, 80 rect REMARKS: Kit. Plug-in coils.

MODEL: All-Star, Jr. (Variation) REMARKS: A later model incorporated regeneration in the IF stage.